W9-CRJ-075

Hedgebrook Cookbook

celebrating radical hospitality

Denise Barr and Julie Rosten

edited by Liz Engelman

SWP

SHE WRITES PRESS

Hedgebrook Cookbook: Celebrating Radical Hospitality

SHE WRITES PRESS
1563 Solano Ave, #546
Berkeley, CA 94707

Published 2013
Printed in China
16 15 14 13 1 2 3 4 5

ISBN: 978-1-938314-22-3
Library of Congress Control Number: 2013940055

Cover design by Julie Valin
Cover concept by Denise Barr
Interior design by Tabitha Lahr
Illustrations by Julie Rosten

To all the women who have gathered around Hedgebrook's farmhouse table
and to all those yet to come.

Contents

Foreword

I've experienced the truth of the Hedgebrook phrase "radical hospitality." It's an umbrella of care that covers such things as fruits, vegetables, and flowers straight from the garden, and the attention given to preserving the long stretches of undisturbed hours that writers crave. But I think even that phrase doesn't quite do justice to the thoughtfulness and ability to notice detail. Now that I'm home again and being asked by friends, I find myself describing Hedgebrook this way: It's as if women took our 5000 years or so of nurturing experience, and turned it on each other.

Only that accounts for the care in constructing cottages that are separate and completely private, yet not so distant from each other that there isn't just the light or the roof of another cottage in view; thus each writer knows that being solitary isn't the same as being isolated. Or the fact that the cook joins the conversation and the table at dinner, so we not only get to know each other, but writers who are used to serving others aren't made to feel uncomfortable by being served.

Many males grow up with a focused view, and many females have a wide view that includes more detail. It's a cultural truth. Even women who don't have children have been raised to value the qualities children need, from attention to detail to patience and empathy. That's not universal, but it is one of the most reliable gender differences. Hedgebrook is a place where women learn to focus on our work. It's also a place where we learn to accept the care we've been trained to give.

—Gloria Steinem

Introduction

The ethos of radical hospitality runs deep in the marrow of Hedgebrook's mission. Nurturing a writer so that she can do her best work is a value that has been flourishing at Hedgebrook for twenty-five years, and counting.

When Nancy Nordhoff founded Hedgebrook in 1988 with her friend Sheryl Feldman, their vision was to support the individual writer through simple acts of generosity: providing her with a beautiful cottage in which to live and work in solitude, connecting her to the land, teaching her to build a fire in her woodstove, feeding her from the organic garden, inviting her to the Farmhouse table each evening to share a home-cooked meal and her stories with other women writers from around the world.

What makes this simple act radical is its manifold impact.

As women, we are used to being the nurturers. We make sure others are fed, clothed and taken care of. We enable their work and visions, sometimes at the expense of our own.

When we turn the tables and nurture a woman writer—we send a powerful message: you are here to be a writer. Not a mother or wife or partner or daughter. Not even a *woman writer*. A writer.

This message takes hold in the writer and fuels her creative process. When she leaves Hedgebrook, she carries it into the world with her, creating a ripple effect that reaches her family, her community, and all of the readers and audiences who experience her work.

Now, twenty-five years into Hedgebrook's story, and through the stories of the 1,400 writers who have come here, literally millions of people have experienced what we've come to call our "radical hospitality."

As we begin a new chapter in Hedgebrook's life, we are happy to share our radical hospitality with you through this cookbook. We envision the ripple effect growing, as you share these recipes and meals with friends and family, around your tables, for the next twenty-five years, and counting.

—Amy Wheeler, Executive Director & alumna

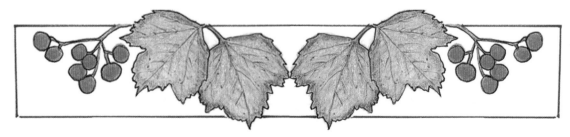

A Note From the Authors

For as far back as I can remember I wanted to be a part of what was going on in the kitchen. Born in the mid-fifties, the kitchen was always for me the heart of feminine energy. The center of that heart belonged to my Nana Carolyn and her sister Cornelia, known by all as Cornie. Their kitchen was the definite "cool club" and I wanted to be a member; not out in the den, watching some football game at Thanksgiving.

Nana and Cornie would be in their kitchen just buzzing after their one glass of pink wine. I would lean against their legs, my arms around their waists, as they laughed out loud trying to unmold a jello salad in the warm water of the sink. I could feel the love they had for each other—and the love they had for me.

They never appeared overwhelmed and the dinners they presented were always spectacular; applause coming from the family as the turkey was set down in the middle of the table. Who could possibly want to be anywhere else?

Fifty years later the kitchen continues to enable me to feel whole. It is what I do with confidence and what I give with love, to others. Hedgebrook has presented me with a gift, a way to stand in my Nana's shoes.

— Denise Barr

My talent for cooking grew from my need to have my family around the dinner table, to enjoy and share meals that strengthen the bonds that make life meaningful. I was born into an Italian-Finnish family and grew up in a predominately Asian neighborhood in South Seattle. I married into a Chinese American family who taught me to cook their dishes. My mother-in-law and her friends would cook for weeks, preparing the appropriate dishes to celebrate the one-month-old birthday parties of each of our children. Two to three hundred people would visit her home, enjoy her food and rub my children's heads with red-dyed eggs for good luck.

Relationships, studies, and work have allowed me sojourns to France, China, Bimini, Italy, Japan, Mexico and across many states of the U.S. I have truly lived and learned to cook in the "multicultural salad bowl" of North America. In all these cultures, the use of food to create community is predominant. Here at Hedgebrook, I am able to showcase my own art form of food preparation and presentation, striving to make each guest feel comforted by my meals. When I left Seattle for Whidbey Island, I told myself it was to get closer to Nature; I didn't realize it was to find my way back to the community that I have always belonged to.

— Julie Rosten

A Hedgebrook Grace

As we prepare to receive this food,
we give thanks to the women
who have fed us through time,
handing down their knowledge
of all that abides in this meal
to nourish and sustain us.

May we, together with all beings,
receive this gift of many lives,
with gratitude and the understanding that
in this meal is the entire world,
and in this world we are one.

— Ruth Ozeki

In The Hedgebrook Garden

I am here to gather what I didn't know
    I desired, bent to earth,
the cat presenting one grey haunch in greeting

and wondering at my hand in the
    strawberry patch searching for early
treasure. She begs to roll like a grub

in the soil, mercy ushering such deep
    thanks through her belly, as if suddenly
here were her life's abundance

laid out in the kale and what she came
    to kill or catch were better left to the wild
uncertainty of this moment, spines of lavender

arching under my hand and the summer
    orchard blooming with gifts. Do not ask
what sound she made, for you already

know it: today, even the blue columbines
    spill with wind and bend their horns
to listen. There is a woman

in the kitchen humming over a pot of greens,
    garlic snaps in oil, the black dog naps
to chase a rabbit through the dark

brush of her dream—
    and this afternoon, you too
will sit at the long wooden table

whose face is worn to luster,
    this table which is your life,
and whose guests say to you now, *Come, eat.*

— Susan B. Anthony Somers-Willett

ONE: WRITER'S PANTRY

Vegan Granola

Makes about 8 cups

4 C rolled oats
2 C shredded coconut (unsweetened)
2 C almonds, coarsely chopped
¾ C dried cranberries
¾ C raisins
¾ C canola oil
¾ C agave nectar
1 tsp ground cinnamon

Preheat oven to 350 degrees.

In large bowl, toss together oats, coconut, almonds, cranberries and raisins.

In a separate small bowl combine canola oil, agave nectar and cinnamon. Stir well. Pour wet ingredients over dry ingredients and mix completely together with your hands or a large wooden spoon until evenly coated.

Spread onto two 12 x 16 inch baking sheets lined with parchment paper.

Bake stirring occasionally with a spatula, until mixture is an even golden brown color, about 12 to 15 minutes.

Chocolate Shortbread Cookies

Makes about 3 dozen

1½ C flour
½ C unsweetened cocoa*
¼ tsp coarse salt
½ pound (2 sticks) unsalted butter,
   room temperature
½ C granulated sugar
1 T cacao nibs*

In a small bowl, sift flour and cocoa together. Add coarse salt and set aside.

With an electric mixer beat butter on medium speed for 3 to 5 minutes until fluffy. Add sugar and cacao nibs and continue to beat until very light in color, about 2 minutes more. Add the flour and cocoa mixture and combine on low speed, until flour is just incorporated and dough sticks together when squeezed with fingers.

On a sheet of wax paper, pat and form the dough into a log about 12 to 14 inches long and 1 to 1½ inches in diameter. If you want a square or rectangular cookie rather than round, flatten each side of the log as you roll it up in the wax paper. Chill until firm, at least 1 hour.

Preheat oven to 325 degrees.

Line a cookie sheet with parchment. Remove the wax paper from the dough and slice the log into ¼ inch thick slices. Lay cookies on lined baking sheets. Bake until firm, 17 to 20 minutes. Cool completely on wire racks. Can be stored in an airtight container for 3 to 4 weeks.

* Use a high quality chocolate such as Scharffen Berger.

Lavender Shortbread Cookies

Makes about 3 dozen

2 C flour
¼ tsp coarse salt
½ pound (2 sticks) unsalted butter,
    room temperature
½ C granulated sugar
1 tsp pure vanilla extract
1 tsp culinary lavender buds

In a small bowl sift flour, add coarse salt and set aside.

Beat butter on medium speed in an electric mixer for 3 to 5 minutes until fluffy. Add sugar, vanilla and lavender buds and continue to beat until very light in color, about 2 minutes more. Add the flour and salt mixture and combine on low speed until flour is just incorporated and dough sticks together when squeezed with fingers.

On a sheet of wax paper, pat and form the dough into a log about 12 to 14 inches long and 1 to 1½ inches in diameter. If you want a square or rectangular cookie rather than round, flatten each side of the log as you roll it up in the wax paper. Chill until firm, at least 1 hour.

Preheat oven to 325 degrees.

Line a cookie sheet with parchment. Remove the wax paper from the dough and slice the log into ¼ inch thick slices. Lay cookies onto lined baking sheets. Bake until firm, 17 to 20 minutes. Cool completely on wire racks. Can be stored in an airtight container for 3 to 4 weeks.

Double Ginger Cookies

Makes 4 dozen

1 C crystallized ginger, divided
1 C sugar, divided
8 T butter, softened
¼ C dark molasses
1 large egg
2 C flour
2 tsp baking soda
1 T ground ginger
¾ tsp cinnamon
½ tsp ground clove
½ tsp ground nutmeg

Preheat oven to 350 degrees.

In food processor add ½ C crystallized ginger and ⅓ C sugar. Process until ginger is finely ground. Add ⅓ C sugar and butter then beat until fluffy. Add molasses and egg to ginger mixture and process until combined. Place mixture in a large mixing bowl. Chop remaining ½ C ginger by hand and add to mixture. In a separate bowl sift together flour, soda, ground ginger, cinnamon, clove and nutmeg. Add to ginger mixture and blend well. Place dough in refrigerator until well chilled, at least one hour

Place the remaining ⅓ C sugar in a shallow dish. Shape dough into one-inch balls roll in sugar to coat. Place on parchment covered cookie sheet, 2 to 3 inches apart. Flatten each ball with the bottom of a juice glass. Bake at 350 degrees for about 7 to 8 minutes.

Cookies should remain soft and chewy.

Toasted Sesame Cookies

Makes about 4 ½ dozen

1 C butter, softened
1 C brown sugar
¾ C white sugar
2 eggs
1¾ C sifted flour
1 tsp salt
1 C sesame seeds, toasted

Preheat oven to 350 degrees.

Toast sesame seeds in a dry skillet over medium heat. Stir frequently and toast until light brown. Let cool.

Cream together butter and sugars in an electric mixer until well blended. Add eggs and mix well after each addition. Add flour, salt and sesame seeds and mix until incorporated.

Place rounded teaspoonfuls on parchment lined baking sheet. Bake for 10 to 12 minutes. If you like them more crisp, bake a little longer.

Upon arrival, you will notice how beautiful Hedgebrook is, how welcoming the people are, how abundant the garden, immaculate and interesting the kitchen, peaceful the forest. You will make yourself at home in your cabin and *slowly* you will slow down. You will meet other women, and you will find that you are as relaxed, as happy, as supported by these others as you have ever been by the many friends you've made over the years. You'll sit down to write every morning, or every night, and a great realization will take hold: that everything around you—forest, footpaths, woodstoves, walls—have kept watch over the work of other women, have absorbed their energies and struggles, and most of all, have absorbed what you are most feeling yourself by the end: gratitude. And you also think about the people working quietly around you—the other women writers, the woodcutters and gardeners and chefs, the people in the office, all working from well before you arrived to well after you depart, to make your writing possible, and because of this, it *is* possible.

—Carolyn Forché

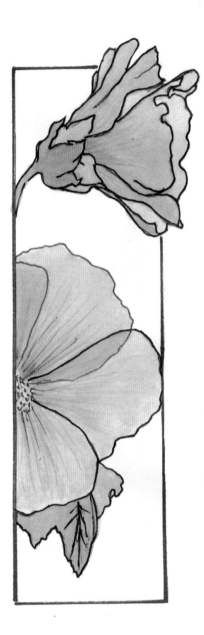

Chewy Fruit Cookies

Makes 3 to 4 dozen

1 C butter, softened
1 C brown sugar
½ C sugar
2 eggs
1 tsp vanilla
1½ C flour
1 tsp baking soda
½ tsp cinnamon
½ tsp salt
2 C oats
½ C raisins
½ C dried apricots, chopped
½ C cranberries
½ C prunes, chopped
½ C shredded coconut

Preheat oven to 350 degrees.

In a large mixing bowl cream together butter, brown sugar and sugar. Mix until fluffy. Add eggs and vanilla and stir well. In a smaller bowl, combine flour, soda, cinnamon and salt and add to wet mixture and stir well. Add all the remaining ingredients and mix well.

Drop rounded spoonfuls of the dough onto a parchment covered cookie sheet. Bake for 10 to 12 minutes.

Gluten-Free Oatmeal Bars

Makes 16-20 squares

Crust:
⅔ C brown rice flour
½ tsp xanthan gum
½ C brown sugar, packed
⅓ C butter
¾ C rolled gluten-free oats

Topping:
¾ C brown sugar, packed
2 T brown rice flour
½ tsp salt
¼ tsp baking powder
2 large eggs, beaten
1 tsp vanilla
½ C nuts, chopped
powdered sugar

Preheat oven to 350 degrees.

Crust: Mix flour, xanthan, and brown sugar. Cut in butter, mix in oats. Press into a 9 x 9 inch pan. Bake 15 minutes.

Topping: Mix brown sugar, flour, salt, baking powder, vanilla and eggs, blend well. Add nuts. Pour over hot crust and tip pan to spread evenly. Cook for another 15 minutes.

Let cool, sprinkle with powdered sugar and cut into squares.

Spicy Caramel Corn

Makes 8 cups

8 C popped corn
1 T butter
1½ C brown sugar
⅓ C agave nectar
1 tsp baking powder
½ tsp kosher salt
¼ to ½ tsp cayenne pepper to taste

Preheat oven to 250 degrees.

Place popped popcorn on large rimmed baking sheet covered with parchment paper. Place in oven while you prepare the caramel.

In a medium saucepan, melt butter, brown sugar and agave over medium heat. Stir only once when butter is melted. Turn heat up to medium high and boil without stirring for 3 minutes or until temperature reaches 250 degrees on a candy thermometer. Immediately remove from heat, and stir in baking powder, salt and cayenne.

Remove baking sheet from oven, and pour caramel over popcorn. Using a fork, mix popcorn with caramel until all pieces are coated. Re-spread evenly on baking sheet, and bake 45 minutes, stirring every 15 minutes. Cool, and store in airtight container.

I had a glimmer of Hedgebrook's nurturing ways when I was told, despite my pleading, that I couldn't bring my dog with me. The voice on the phone kindly but firmly explained that for ten days I wasn't going to take care of anything besides myself. For a mother of two with a full-time job and a weekly newspaper column, this alone was revelatory.

Still, I had no idea what radical hospitality meant until I'd spent a night alone in a cabin that held me snug as a turtle's shell, spent a day and then the next day in solitude and forest quiet, and ate food picked fresh from the earth at the communal table.

Hedgebrook's island setting, the towering hush of its native conifers, can be daunting for writers from big cities or parts of the world less deeply green than our own. The open orchard and sunny vegetable garden, its tidy raised beds and abandon of flowers, is comfortingly familiar to women away from home. At Hedgebrook, the connections between earth and table, between humans and trees, between body and soul, are cultivated as skillfully as the soil in the organic vegetable patch.

How intimidated can you be by the big work of writing when you're given a pair of clippers and a vase and invited to cut flowers, to snack on sun-warmed raspberries fresh from the vine, to hang out among the cornstalks and buzzing bees?

Hedgebrook blurs the lines between nature outside of us and within us. The land, trees, garden, the cocoon of quiet, freedom from routine and responsibilities all merge at Hedgebrook—seeming magically, but actually quite calculatedly—to gently propel the writer along her path.

— Valerie Easton

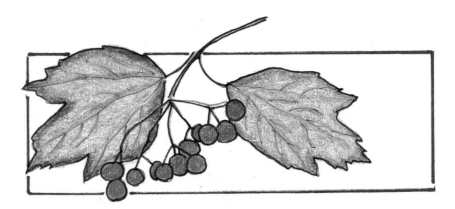

Candied Almonds

Makes 2 cups

3 T peanut oil
2 C whole almonds, blanched
½ C plus 1 T sugar, divided
1½ tsp kosher salt
1½ tsp ground cumin
1 tsp red pepper flakes

Place almonds in bowl and pour boiling water over to cover. Let sit 1 minute and no longer or else the almonds won't be crisp. Drain and rinse in cold water and drain again. Pat dry and squeeze skins off.

Heat oil in a heavy frying pan over medium-high heat. Add the almonds and sprinkle the ½ cup sugar over them. Sauté until the almonds are golden brown and the sugar caramelizes.

Remove almonds from the pan and toss in a bowl with the salt, cumin, pepper flakes and remaining tablespoon of sugar.

Serve warm or at room temperature. Store in an airtight container.

Gingered Pecans

Makes 5 cups

5 C pecan halves
½ C sugar
2 tsp kosher salt
1 tsp ground ginger
2 T honey
2 tsp canola oil

Heat oven to 325 degrees.

Spread the nuts in single layers on two rimmed cookie sheets. Toast until the nuts are fragrant about 10 to 15 minutes. While the nuts are toasting, combine the sugar, salt, and ginger in a small bowl and set aside.

Combine honey, 2 tablespoons of water, and the oil in a large saucepan and bring to a boil over high heat. Reduce to medium and pour in the hot pecans and stir until all the liquid has evaporated about 2 to 3 minutes. Transfer the nuts to a large bowl and add the sugar, ginger mixture and toss until all the nuts are coated.

Spread the nuts onto a piece of parchment paper in a single layer and let cool. Store up to one week in an airtight container at room temperature.

TWO: SUNDAY BRUNCH

Ginger Pumpkin Bread

Makes 2 loaves

3 C sugar
½ C butter, softened
½ C canola oil
4 eggs
⅔ C buttermilk
2 C cooked pumpkin or any sweet
   winter squash*
3½ C flour
2 tsp baking soda
1 tsp baking powder
½ tsp salt
2 tsp ground ginger
1 tsp ground cinnamon
1 tsp ground nutmeg
1 tsp ground cloves
1 tsp ground allspice
8 oz crystallized ginger, chopped
1 C pecans, chopped

Preheat oven 350 degrees.

In a large bowl beat sugar and butter until light in color. Add oil, eggs, and buttermilk and mix well. Mix in pumpkin.

In a separate bowl sift together flour, baking soda, baking powder and salt. Add ground ginger, cinnamon, nutmeg, cloves, and allspice, and mix well. Pour dry ingredients into the pumpkin mixture and stir until blended. Add crystallized ginger and nuts.

Pour into two greased 9-inch loaf pans. Bake up to 1 hour. Test for doneness with a toothpick.

* 16 oz canned pumpkin is okay.

Vegan Pumpkin Bread

Makes three 7 x 3 inch loaf pans

3½ C flour
3 C sugar
2 tsp baking soda
1 tsp cinnamon
1 tsp nutmeg
1 tsp salt
1 C canola oil
2 C pumpkin
⅔ C water
½ C nuts, chopped
½ C raisins

Preheat oven to 350 degrees.

In a large mixing bowl, sift together dry ingredients. In a separate bowl combine oil, pumpkin and water. Form a hole in the center of the flour mixture and pour in the oil and pumpkin mixture. Mix well and add nuts and raisins.

Grease and flour pans. Pour batter into the pans. Bake for 50 to 60 minutes. Test for doneness with a toothpick.

Anne's Muffins

Make about 15 muffins

1½ C unbleached flour
¾ C flaxseed meal (flaxseeds pulverized in a grinder)
¾ C oat bran (rolled oats pulverized in a grinder)
1 C brown sugar (not packed)
1 tsp baking powder
½ tsp salt
2 tsp cinnamon
1½ C carrots, shredded
2 medium apples, grated
½ C raisins or other dried fruit (cranberries, apricots, cherries)
1 C walnuts, chopped
¾ C milk
2 eggs, beaten
1 tsp vanilla

Preheat oven to 350 degrees.

Mix dry ingredients together in a large bowl. Add carrots, apple, raisins, and walnuts to the flour mixture. In separate bowl, combine milk, beaten eggs and vanilla. Add milk mixture to the flour mixture. Stir just until moistened. Do not overmix.

Line muffin tins with cupcake papers, or spray the tins with a cooking spray. Fill tins ¾ to the top. Bake for 15 to 20 minutes. Cool muffins in the tins.

On Radical Hospitality

Perhaps the most beautiful thing about Hedgebrook is its subtlety—the things you don't even notice unless you stop and look. The way your cabin is situated in order to look out on a graceful maple tree, your location within calling distance, but never sight, of the woman living next door. The way you have just enough of a kitchen to make tea, but not enough to claim your hands or mind with food preparation. The way, at the end of the day, you walk through the woods of your mind to the bright light of the farmhouse, where people and food await. The way the farmhouse table is part of, but not in, the kitchen; and the living room, where you go after dinner to read your work, is filled with big, enveloping chairs for those who need to curl up, window seats for those who like a view.

You learn things here—to believe in yourself, and your writing. You make your own fire, create your own heat. You make your own schedule and learn to follow the rhythms of your thoughts. And sometime, maybe even on the last day, you look out the window and realize you have slowed down enough to see that someone placed your cabin just so, facing a tree you might never have noticed otherwise.

— Erica Bauermeister

Blueberry Scones

Makes 8 scones

2 C flour
1½ tsp cream of tartar
¾ tsp baking soda
½ tsp salt
2-3 T sugar (to taste)
8 T cold butter, cut into 16 pieces
½ C blueberries (frozen)
½ C milk (or more if needed)
1 egg
sugar for topping

Preheat oven to 400 degrees.

In a small bowl combine flour, cream of tartar, baking soda, salt and sugar. Put cold pieces of butter into a food processor with a steel blade. Add the flour mixture all at once and pulse just until mixed. You should still see some bits of butter. (This can be done by hand using a pastry blender.) Turn butter and flour mixture into a bowl. Gently stir frozen blueberries into the flour mixture by hand.

In a separate bowl, mix milk and the egg together. Hold out 2 tablespoons of this mixture to brush on top of scones later. Add milk and egg mixture to the flour mixture and gently mix together with your hands until just incorporated, trying not to smash up the frozen blueberries too much. If dough does not stick together, add a little more milk one tablespoon at a time.

Turn dough out onto a floured surface and divide the dough into two balls. Gently flatten one ball into a disk and dust lightly with flour. Fold in half and reshape into a mound. Repeat with second ball of dough. Brush the egg wash on the top of each mound and sprinkle with coarse sugar, if desired. Cut each mound into four wedges.

Place the eight scones with ample room between them, on an ungreased baking sheet. Bake for 12 to 15 minutes.

Banana Cardamom Bread

Makes a 9-inch loaf pan

¾ C currants
⅓ C dark rum
1¾ C flour
2 tsp baking powder
1 tsp baking soda
½ tsp salt
1 tsp ground cardamom
3 ripe bananas, mashed
⅓ C canola oil
¾ C brown sugar
2 eggs
½ C walnuts, chopped

Preheat oven to 350 degrees.

In small saucepan combine currants and rum. Bring to a simmer, turn off heat and let pan sit for 15 minutes. Meanwhile in a medium bowl, combine flour, baking powder, soda, salt and cardamom. Mix well and set aside.

Mash bananas and put in large mixing bowl. Add oil and brown sugar and beat for a few minutes using electric mixer. Add eggs and beat another minute. Add flour mixture to wet ingredients and mix until just combined. By hand stir in walnuts, soaked currants and their liquid.

Spoon into greased 9 inch loaf pan. Bake approximately 1 hour 15 minutes. Test for doneness with a toothpick.

Baked French Toast

Serves 8 to 10

1 baguette (24 inch long)
6 eggs
2 C milk
1 C brown sugar, divided
½ tsp nutmeg
1 tsp vanilla
4 T butter
pinch of salt
½ C cream
1 C pecans

Preheat oven to 350 degrees.

Generously butter a 9 x 13 inch baking dish. Cut 1-inch thick slices from baguette and arrange in one layer in buttered baking dish.

Whisk together eggs, milk, ¾ C brown sugar, nutmeg and vanilla in large bowl until well combined. Pour evenly over bread. Let bread soak for 10 minutes. Turn slices over and cover pan with plastic wrap. Place a baking dish on top to keep bread submerged. Refrigerate until all liquid is absorbed—overnight or at least 8 hours. Remove from refrigerator one hour prior to baking.

Combine butter and remaining ¼ C brown sugar, salt, and cream in a small saucepan. Bring just to a boil, stirring until sugar is dissolved. Stir in pecans. Spoon pecan mixture over bread.

Bake until bread is puffed and edges are lightly brown and liquid is absorbed, about 40 to 45 minutes. Serve with syrup.

Tomato Tart

Serves 6 to 8

Crust:
1¼ C flour
½ C Gruyere cheese, grated
1½ tsp dried thyme
½ tsp kosher salt
½ tsp sugar
½ C butter, cold, and cut into little pieces
2 to 4 T ice water
1 egg
1 tsp water

Filling:
1 T olive oil
1 medium onion, diced
3 to 4 garlic cloves, minced
3 T flour
2 lbs grape tomatoes
½ C fresh basil, chopped
1½ tsp kosher salt
1½ tsp pepper

Crust: Add flour, cheese, thyme, salt and sugar together in a food processor. Pulse a few times to mix. Add butter and pulse until incorporated, 8 to 15 seconds. Add ice water, a tablespoon at a time, just until dough begins to form (it will still be crumbly, but will stick together if pinched). Turn out dough into a large bowl, and work into a disk, about 1 inch thick. Wrap in plastic wrap and refrigerate 20 to 30 minutes.

Preheat oven to 375 degrees.

Filling: Sauté onion in olive oil over medium heat for 8 to 10 minutes, until translucent. Add garlic and cook for 1 minute. Take off heat and let cool. In a large bowl, combine onion and garlic, and sprinkle with flour. Add grape tomatoes, basil, salt, pepper and mix to coat.

Pour mixture into pie pan, piling up the tomatoes (they will cook down). Roll out crust just a bit larger than the pie pan, and cover tomato mixture, tucking under the edges. Crimp edges to seal. Beat egg with a fork and mix in 1 tsp water. Brush this mixture over the crust. Cut 5 slits in the pie for venting.

Bake for 45 to 50 minutes, until tomatoes are bubbling and top is golden brown. (Cover pie with foil while baking if top browns too quickly.) Tip: The tomatoes tend to bubble over during cooking, so you can place a foil-lined tray on rack below, to catch tomato juice as it cooks. Let stand on wire rack to cool to room temperature, about an hour.

Chard Frittata

Serves 6 to 8

1 T olive oil
2 bunches chard (approximately 1 C
   cooked)
4 large cloves garlic, finely chopped
1 red pepper, roasted, diced
4 green onions, thinly sliced
½ C grated pecorino romano
   (or parmesan)
4 oz goat feta, crumbled
1 tsp fresh rosemary, finely chopped
2 tsp lemon juice
10 eggs, beaten
½ tsp salt
¼ tsp pepper
pinch of red pepper flakes (optional)

Preheat oven to 350 degrees.

Remove ribs and stems from chard. Steam chard, drain, cool and squeeze out any excess water and coarsely chop. Sauté garlic in olive oil and set aside.

Place chard in a bowl with red pepper, green onions, pecorino romano, feta, sautéed garlic, rosemary, lemon juice, eggs, salt, pepper and red pepper flakes. Mix gently.

Coat a 9-inch glass pie pan lightly with oil and add mixture to pan. Bake about 30 minutes or until eggs are firm in center. Allow to set before serving.

Savory Galette

Cornmeal Crust:

Makes 2 crusts

2 C flour

½ C cornmeal

1 tsp salt

1 tsp sugar

1 C unsalted butter, cold, cut into small pieces

¼ to ½ C ice water

Delicata Squash Filling:

Makes enough filling for one 15-inch Galette

2 tsp butter

1 T honey

1 delicata squash*, unpeeled, cut into ½ inch rounds and seeded

coarse salt

freshly ground pepper

3 T olive oil

1 onion, thinly sliced

1 disk of galette dough

flour for work surface

1 pound fresh ricotta cheese

3 large eggs, (one saved for egg wash)

12 fresh sage leaves

Crust: In a food processor pulse together flour, cornmeal, salt and sugar. Add cubed butter pieces and process about 10 seconds, until butter is evenly distributed. Pulse processor while adding just enough ice water so dough holds together. Do not process more than 30 seconds.

Turn dough out on a floured surface and knead dough with your hands to form two equal disks. Wrap each disk in plastic wrap and refrigerate at least 1 hour or up to one day (you can freeze wrapped dough for later use).

Delicata Squash Filling: Preheat oven to 450 degrees.

Melt butter and honey in small pan and brush onto both cut sides of the squash. Arrange squash in single layer on baking sheet and season with salt and pepper. Bake until rounds are browned on the bottom, about 15 minutes. Set aside.

In large skillet with olive oil, sauté onion over medium-low heat. Cook slowly, stirring occasionally until onions caramelize, about 15 to 20 minutes. In medium bowl stir together ricotta cheese and 2 eggs. Season with salt and pepper, set aside.

Roll dough into a 15 inch circle on a piece of floured parchment and transfer dough, with parchment, to a

(continued on next page)

(continued from previous page)

rimmed baking sheet. Spread ricotta mixture onto center of dough leaving a 1-inch border. Evenly scatter the caramelized onions and place the delicata rounds in a single layer over the ricotta filling. Sprinkle with sage leaves, salt and pepper. Fold dough over the edge of the filling to form a pleated rustic crust. Refrigerate galette 20 to 30 minutes.

Preheat oven to 375 degrees.

To make the egg wash beat remaining egg with 1 tablespoon of cold water and brush over crust. Bake until golden brown about 50 to 60 minutes. Cut into wedges. Serve warm or at room temperature.

* Other types of squash can be used as long as they are peeled and precooked. We have spooned dollops of baked hubbard, red kuri or butternut squash onto the galette instead of using delicata slices.

Spinach Pie

Serves 6 to 8

3 C yellow onions, chopped
2 T olive oil
2 tsp salt
1½ tsp pepper
4 lbs spinach*, steamed, drained and
  chopped
6 eggs, beaten
2 tsp nutmeg
½ C parmesan cheese, grated
3 T breadcrumbs
½ lb feta cut into half-inch cubes
8 T salted butter, melted
6-8 sheets phyllo dough

Preheat oven to 375 degrees.

Sauté onions in olive oil on medium heat for 10 to 15 minutes. Add salt and pepper. Let cool.

Steam or wilt spinach in large covered pot with a small amount of water. Drain spinach and let cool. Squeeze out excess water and chop coarsely. In large bowl beat eggs, add spinach, onions, nutmeg, parmesan, feta and breadcrumbs.

Butter a 9½ inch oven proof pie plate. Line pie plate with 6 sheets of phyllo dough brushing butter between each sheet. Let each layer extend out over edge of plate. Pour egg mixture in middle. Fold over edges of phyllo onto middle of pie. Brush top with butter. Add one or two more sheets of phyllo dough crumpled on top of pie.

Bake 1 hour until filling is set. Allow to cool completely. Cut into wedges and serve.

*Frozen spinach works well, use 3 (10 oz) packages, thawed and drained.

The frogs are singing now at Hedgebrook. It's downright brazen stuff. We asked Hedgebrook's gardener Cathy Bruemmer what they were singing about and she said, with a little lift of the shoulders, "Well . . . *love*." Of course. We all listen to it in our cottages. Well, it's not like you can choose. It stops unaccountably every now and then, and the silence is deafening. We all listen to that as well. And then, just as mysteriously, for reasons of their own, they start up again, thrumming away for hours at a time. As I write or try to write in my cottage, of course the metaphor is inescapable, the way it flows, stops, holds, then slides into motion again—the desire to sing, the flame of song eating the air, and then the sudden reticence while you wait, pen raised, for the song to return. For reasons of its own and in its own time. In our cottages, listening to the frogs, we all wait; you can see us waiting, lights glowing through the nights, wood smoke trailing in the days, listening to the frogs who sing of love, who sing "now, now, now," and how right they are, because that is what we have, all of us: now. How lucky we are, we who listen.

— Ellen McLaughlin

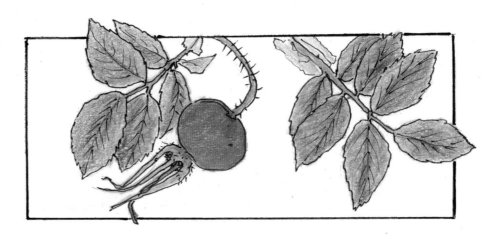

Zucchini Potato Frittata

Serves 6 to 8

1 yellow onion, chopped
2 T olive oil
1 tsp salt
¾ tsp pepper
1 zucchini, sliced into ¼ inch rounds
1 T lemon zest
1 potato, quartered lengthwise and cut
    into ¼ inch slices
8 eggs, beaten
2 T butter
¼ C parmesan cheese, grated
¼ C pine nuts

In an oven proof 12-inch skillet, sauté onion in olive oil on medium-low heat for about 10 to 15 minutes until caramelized and edges are browning. Add salt and pepper. Let cool in skillet.

In a small pot of boiling water, blanch the zucchini slices and zest of one lemon for 1 minute; remove zucchini and zest with strainer or slotted spoon and set aside to cool. Using the same boiling water, add potato slices and boil for 2 to 3 minutes until almost done, drain and let cool.

In a medium size bowl beat the eggs with a wire whisk. Return the skillet with the onions to medium heat and place zucchini and potato slices and lemon zest evenly in a single layer on top of the onions. Add 2 tablespoons of butter to the skillet. When the pan is hot and the butter starts to bubble, pour the beaten egg mixture over the zucchini and potato slices. Let the frittata cook for a minute or two and turn down the heat. With a fork, lift the egg that is starting to cook on the bottom of the skillet and let the runny egg fill in underneath. Keep lifting all around the pan until there is very little runny egg left on top. Be sure to keep the heat low during this process so the bottom of the frittata doesn't burn.

Sprinkle grated parmesan and pine nuts over the top of the frittata and place under a broiler to finish cooking the top. It will only take a few minutes to firm up any runny egg and brown the pine nuts and parmesan. Cut into wedges and serve warm or at room temperature.

Baked Chile Rellenos with Pico de Gallo

Serves 6

Chile Rellenos:
6 fresh poblano chilies, charred, peeled,
   and seeded
4 oz jack cheese, cut into six strips
4 eggs
⅓ C milk
½ C flour
½ tsp baking powder
1 C sharp cheddar cheese, shredded

Pico de Gallo:
3 tomatoes, diced
½ medium onion, diced
¼ bunch of cilantro (use more or less
   depending on your taste)
juice of one lime
1 tsp of salt
2 jalapenos, seeded and finely minced

Chile Rellenos: Preheat oven to 375 degrees.

Char fresh chilies over an open flame or in a broiler. When completely blackened, hold under cold running water and rub gently with fingertips removing charred skin. Make a small incision in the top of the chile to remove stem, seeds and pith leaving chilies whole. Stuff each chile with a strip of jack cheese. Arrange chilies side by side in the bottom of a greased shallow 1½ qt baking dish.

Beat eggs until thick and foamy, then add milk, flour and baking powder; beat until smooth as possible. Pour egg batter evenly over chilies. Sprinkle with cheddar cheese.

Bake uncovered for about 30 minutes or until casserole is puffed and appears set when gently shaken. Serve at once with Pico de Gallo and sour cream.

Pico de Gallo: Mix all ingredients together in a bowl.

THREE: LUNCH BOX

SOUPS

Clam Chowder

47

Carrot Ginger Orange

48

Tomato Cocount

49

Chicken Tortilla

51

Hot and Sour

54

Zucchini Bisque

55

Ginger Broth with Sweet Potato

57

Clam Chowder

Serves 6 to 8

6 oz uncured smoked bacon, chopped
1 large yellow onion, diced
2 bay leaves
½ red bell pepper, diced
2 stalks celery, cut once length wise
   and thinly sliced
4 C potatoes, peeled and cubed
   (yellow or red)
¼ C parsley, chopped
2 pinches red chili flakes, to taste
1 large (51 oz) can of clams, separated
   (which is approximately 3½ C of
   juice and 3½ C of clams)
4 C half and half
salt and pepper to taste
smoked paprika (optional)

Brown bacon, over medium heat, in a large, heavy-bottomed stockpot. When bacon is crisp, remove with slotted spoon and set aside. Add the onion and bay leaves to the stockpot with the rendered bacon fat. Cook slowly until the onions start to brown, about 10 minutes. Add the bell pepper, celery, potatoes, parsley and chili flakes, sauté for another minute or two.

Add the clam juice (from the canned clams) to the stockpot, reserving the clams to add later. Bring the chowder to a slow simmer over medium low heat and cook until potatoes are tender. Add the clams, half and half, reserved bacon, salt and pepper, and heat through without bringing to a boil. Serve warm with a sprinkle of smoked paprika.

Carrot Ginger Orange Soup

Serves 6 to 8

5 C vegetable stock
1 T olive oil
1 medium yellow onion, chopped
4 cloves garlic
1 T fresh ginger grated
1½ tsp ground cumin
1 tsp ground coriander
¼ tsp cayenne pepper
2 lbs carrots, thinly sliced
1 medium sweet potato, peeled,
    chopped
½ C orange juice (more if soup needs
    to be thinned a bit)
salt and pepper to taste
cilantro, finely chopped

Heat oil in heavy stockpot, add onion and sauté over medium heat until onion becomes translucent. Add garlic, cumin, coriander, ginger and cayenne. Cook until onion is soft. Add carrots, sweet potato and stock. Cover and simmer until carrots are very tender about 20 minutes.

Purée soup until smooth. Add orange juice and salt and pepper to taste. Garnish with a sprinkle of cilantro.

Tomato Coconut Soup

Serves 6 to 8

3 T olive oil
½ large yellow onion, chopped
4 large cloves garlic, finely chopped
2 T ginger root, peeled, finely chopped
   (2 to 3 inch piece)
1 jalapeño pepper, seeded, minced
3 bay leaves
2 celery ribs, chopped
½ green bell pepper, chopped
1 tsp dry basil
2 cans (28 oz each) fire roasted whole
   tomatoes
2 cans (14 oz each) coconut milk
fresh basil

Heat oil in large heavy pot, sauté onions for a few minutes. Add garlic, ginger, jalapeño and bay; cook over low heat until onions are soft and translucent.

Blend one can of tomatoes in blender until liquefied and add to pot. Drain the juice from the second can into pot, chop remaining tomatoes and add to pot. Add celery, bell pepper and dry basil. Cook until peppers and celery are soft. Add coconut milk and heat through.

Serve in individual bowls with plenty of fresh chopped basil for the top.

Chicken Tortilla Soup

Serves 6 to 8

2 T olive oil
1 medium onion, chopped
3 cloves garlic, minced
2 boneless skinless chicken breasts,
  chopped into ½ inch cubes
2 tsp California chili powder (or any
  mild chili powder)
¼ tsp chipotle chili powder (optional)
1 tsp oregano
1 tsp cumin
1 can (28 oz) diced tomatoes (fire roasted)
1 qt chicken broth
1 C corn
1 C white hominy
1 can (4 oz) chopped mild green chilies
2 fresh pasilla chilies, blackened,
  skinned, cleaned and chopped
1 can (14½ oz) pinto beans, drained
⅓ C sliced black olives

Toppings:
avocado, chopped
jack cheese, shredded
green onions, chopped
cilantro, chopped
sour cream
tortilla chips, crushed

In a large heavy pot add olive oil, onion and garlic, sauté until lightly brown. Add chicken cubes and continue cooking until chicken browns. Add chili powders, oregano, cumin, tomatoes and chicken broth. Continue to simmer until chicken is fully cooked, about 10 minutes. Add the rest of the soup ingredients, continue to simmer until well heated and ready to serve.

Serve in individual bowls; add tortilla chips to the bottom of the bowl, cover with soup and finish off with the toppings of your choice.

Shortly before I came to Hedgebrook, my mother died. I was with her in her final days, caring for her intimately in a way that I hadn't since my own children were born. I also helped plan her funeral, package her ashes, reunite our extended family for her favorite holiday—Thanksgiving—and mourn with my two boys. And before, during, and after this, I published a book, went on a publicity tour, was nominated for an award, and taught creative writing. I had been home no more than five days in a row for five months, and my Hedgebrook residency loomed as one more thing I had to do.

I can only guess what I must have looked like when I arrived because I was taken directly to the farmhouse where Denise and the smell of fresh chocolate chip cookies welcomed me.

I was a motherless mother. It wasn't until that moment, sitting at the farmhouse table with tea and a hot cookie and my luggage still unloaded in the car, that I felt it.

I spent the next three weeks alone in my cabin, with the sound of the frogs, and my crackling fire, and a novel that I had to either wrestle into shape or abandon. But it was the radical hospitality in the farmhouse each night that resuscitated my manuscript: the food made with love and just for me, and a new family of sisters around the table. Hedgebrook was my refuge before I knew I needed one, and the encouragement, support, and friendship I found there followed me home.

—Rahna Reiko Rizzuto

Hot and Sour Soup

Serves 4 to 6

4 C chicken broth, divided
2 T soy sauce
1 oz sliced, dried shiitake mushrooms,
    presoaked
1 can (5 oz) bamboo shoot strips,
    drained
6 oz cooked chicken breast, cubed
6 oz firm tofu, cubed
2 tsp white pepper
¾ C rice vinegar
3 T sesame oil
½ to 1 T Asian chili sauce (Sambal)
    to taste
2 T cornstarch
6 green onions, finely sliced
2 eggs beaten

Cover the dried mushrooms with boiling water and allow to sit 20 to 30 minutes until they have softened, drain and set aside.

Place a large stockpot over medium heat and add 3½ C chicken broth. Add soy sauce, mushrooms, bamboo shoots, chicken, tofu, white pepper, vinegar, sesame oil and chili sauce. Bring to a low simmer, mixing well.

In a small bowl combine remaining ½ C chicken broth and cornstarch, mixing until there are no lumps. Slowly add cornstarch mixture to the soup pot. Stir continuously as the soup thickens and returns to a simmer. Add green onions, stir in the beaten raw eggs and remove from heat and serve.

Zucchini Bisque

Serves 6 to 8

1 medium yellow onion, chopped
½ C butter
2 lbs zucchini, grated
4 C vegetable stock (or chicken stock)
½ tsp nutmeg, freshly grated
1 tsp dry basil
1 tsp salt, to taste (reminder, canned
  stock may have a fair amount of salt)
½ tsp white pepper
1 C heavy cream (optional)

In large saucepan, melt butter and sauté the onion until soft.

Add grated zucchini and vegetable stock, simmer covered for 15 minutes.

Purée soup in a food processor in two separate batches, adding half of the nutmeg, basil, salt and pepper to each batch then combine batches. You may also use an immersion blender directly in the saucepan.

Can be made ahead until this point. When ready to serve, reheat gently and then add cream if desired. Can be served hot or cold.

Ginger Broth with Sweet Potato

Serves 6 to 8

1½ T vegetable oil
½ tsp cumin seeds
1 tsp coriander seeds, crushed
1 tsp yellow mustard seeds
½ tsp tumeric
8 fresh curry leaves
2 inch piece of fresh ginger, peeled
   and julienned
3 garlic cloves, minced
1 small red chili, finely chopped or
   ½ tsp red pepper flakes
4 medium plum tomatoes, crushed
   or diced
7 C vegetable stock
1 tsp salt
1 sweet potato, peeled, sliced into
   ¼ inch thick quarter rounds
lime, cut into wedges
fresh cilantro

Heat oil in large soup pot over medium heat. Add cumin, coriander and mustard seeds. Cook until they start to pop. Add tumeric, curry leaves, ginger, garlic and chili and keep stirring for one minute.

Stir in tomatoes, stock and salt, bring to a boil. Add sweet potato slices and cook until tender, about 10 minutes. Serve with lime wedges and cilantro.

SALADS

Tuscan Kale and Apple

61

Beet and Fennel

63

Quinoa Apricot Almond

64

Nana's Potato Salad

65

Shrimp and Mango

67

Tofu with Napa Cabbage

70

Asparagus Chicken

71

Curried Chicken

73

Tuscan Kale and Apple Salad

Serves 8 to10

1 lb Tuscan kale (also called Dinosaur
   or Lacinato kale)
2 large Honey Crisp apples, unpeeled,
   cored and julienned
Lemon Vinaigrette*

Remove stems and center rib from kale leaves and discard. Stack the leaves on top of one another and cut them crosswise into very thin slices. (Kale should look like thinly shredded cabbage.)

Julienne the apples, using a Benriner (Japanese mandolin) with a coarse blade. You can also do it by hand or use the large holes on a hand held shredder. Put the apple matchsticks immediately into half of the lemon vinaigrette, which will keep the apple from turning brown.

In a large bowl toss the kale and apple with dressing to coat the salad well. Season with salt and pepper to taste. Keep the salad covered and chilled. It is best when it has been dressed and chilled for at least an hour before serving and will hold for a second day.

*See recipe in Chef's Pantry section.

Beet and Fennel Salad

Serves 6 to 8

1 C walnuts
5 to 6 medium size beets
1 large fennel bulb, trimmed, cored,
   and thinly sliced
¼ red onion, thinly sliced
fresh salad greens, or a bed of
   raw spinach
Lemon Vinaigrette*

Preheat oven to 350 degrees.

Toast walnuts in a shallow baking pan and bake until toasted, about 10 minutes.

Cook the beets with their peel on. Cover the beets with water, bring to a boil, and simmer for 30 minutes or until beets can easily be pierced through with a fork. Allow beets to cool and remove peel. Slice into ¼ inch rounds. Place the beets in a small bowl and coat with vinaigrette.

Place the greens on individual plates or on a large shallow serving bowl. Arrange sliced beets on top of the salad greens. Sprinkle fennel and red onion slices on top of beets. Drizzle vinaigrette over entire salad.

*See recipe in Chef's Pantry section.

Quinoa, Apricot and Almond Salad

Serves 4 to 6

1 C quinoa
1 T olive oil
2 C boiling water
4 green onions, thinly sliced
½ C dried apricots, halved and sliced
½ C almonds, toasted and chopped
1 lemon, zest and juice
salt and pepper to taste
Asian Ginger Dressing *

In a heavy medium sauce pan heat oil and add quinoa. Stir quinoa for a few minutes until it starts to brown. Stir in boiling water. Bring to a boil, cover and reduce to a low heat. Allow to simmer for 15 minutes. Remove from heat. Quickly remove lid and cover pan with a clean dish towel and replace lid. Let rest, covered for 30 minutes.

In a large bowl mix warm quinoa with enough dressing to coat the salad. Because the quinoa is warm, it will easily absorb the dressing. Add green onions, apricots, almonds, lemon zest and juice. Add salt and pepper to taste.

Refrigerate salad overnight. Before serving taste to see if salad needs more dressing. Most likely it will have been absorbed and need a little more, but be careful not to overdress.

*See recipe in Chef's Pantry section.

Nana's Potato Salad

Serves 6 to 8

6 to 8 medium Yukon Gold potatoes
½ red onion, diced
2 ribs celery, diced
3 kosher dill pickles, chopped
3 oz sliced black olives
½ red bell pepper, diced
4 T drained capers
¼ C fresh parsley, chopped
2 hard boiled eggs, chopped
¾ C mayonnaise
2 T stone ground mustard
½ tsp dry dill (double if fresh)
salt and pepper to taste
smoked paprika
homemade vinaigrette*

Boil whole potatoes with skins on until tender. Test with a knife tip, making sure they do not become overdone (soft and mushy). Run under cold water and drain. Cut in half and allow to cool. Cube the potatoes into ½ to 1-inch cubes. Place potatoes in large bowl and coat them with the vinaigrette. Add the red onion, celery, dill pickles, olives, red bell pepper, capers and parsley. Mix gently with your hands and set aside.

Combine eggs, mayonnaise, mustard, dill, salt and pepper. Mix well and add to potato mixture. Toss everything together gently. Top with a sprinkling of paprika. This potato salad is best made the day before.

*See Chef's Pantry recipe for Dijon Balsamic Vinaigrette, substitute a white balsamic vinegar for the red.

Shrimp and Mango Salad

Serves 6 to 8

1 lb shrimp, in shells
1 ripe mango, peeled and diced small
1 large ripe tomato, diced small
1 jalapeño, finely diced
½ red onion, finely diced
¼ C chopped cilantro
fresh salad greens
2 T fresh lime juice
1 T olive oil
1 T honey
salt and pepper to taste

Bring a large pot of salted water to a boil. Add shrimp and cook just until they turn bright pink, about 2 to 3 minutes, being careful not to overcook. Drain and place shrimp in ice water to cool. Remove the shells, devein, rinse and let drain well.

In a medium size bowl, combine the shrimp, mango, tomato, jalapeño, onion and cilantro and toss gently to combine. In a small bowl, combine the lime juice, olive oil and honey and whisk until frothy. Pour over salad and toss again to combine. Season to taste with salt and pepper.

Cover bowl and let marinate in the fridge for 1 to 2 hours before serving. If the salad produces too much liquid, strain off some before serving (or serve with a slotted spoon). Serve chilled over fresh greens.

What's A Woman Without Good Stories

travelin inside her travelin round her
what's a woman without good stories feeding her
like mashed potatoes n vinegar greens
fingers n a good mouth at midnight

what's a woman without good stories i ask you

i know a woman go looking for things to feed her
looking in places leave her empty
empty n not knowing why

a woman got ta have good stories
in the kitchen in the street
in the bedroom in the wind

stories make her know which step a good step
how to keep a back straight
n why it's a good idea to keep singing
even when yr purse feels light

—Ruth Forman

Tofu with Napa Cabbage Salad

Serves 8 to10

Baked Tofu:
2 pkg (14 oz each) extra firm tofu,
  drained, blotted, cut into half-inch cubes
1 jalapeño pepper, seeded, minced
3 T fresh ginger, minced
5 cloves garlic, minced
¼ C soy sauce
2 T toasted sesame oil
¼ C sweet Thai chili sauce (Nuoe
  cham ga)

Dressing:
3 T ginger, minced
½ C rice vinegar
1 T agave syrup (or honey)
1½ C canola oil
3 T toasted sesame oil
3 T Dijon mustard
salt and pepper to taste

Salad:
1 large or 2 small heads Napa cabbage,
1 C red onion, thinly sliced
1 red pepper, thinly sliced
2 C bean sprouts
2 to 3 inner stalks of celery including
  leaves, chopped
1/2 bunch cilantro, chopped loosely
1 C pea pods

Preheat oven to 350 degrees.

Baked Tofu: Toss all Baked Tofu ingredients together in a deep baking dish (uncovered) and bake for 1 to 1 ½ hours, stirring occasionally. The tofu should be golden brown and almost crisp. Remove from oven and cool.

Dressing: Place dressing ingredients in jar and shake well.

Salad: In a medium bowl combine cooled tofu with ⅓ of the dressing. Stir gently to coat tofu. Combine all of the salad ingredients together in a large bowl. Add marinated tofu mixture to the salad and toss. Add extra dressing to your taste.

Asparagus Chicken Salad

Serves 6 to 8

1 chicken, quartered
1 lb fresh asparagus
¼ tsp brown sugar
1 large stalk celery, sliced diagonally,
    about ¼ inch wide
1 (2 oz) jar pimientos, drained
2 green onions (white and green part),
    thinly sliced diagonally
fresh basil, chopped (for serving)

Dressing:
⅓ C sour cream
1 tsp dried basil, crushed
3 T capers (with juice)
salt and pepper

Quarter chicken and place in heavy covered pot with enough water to cover bird. Simmer until tender, approximately 45 minutes. Allow to cool in water. Skin, bone and cube chicken, then chill.

In a shallow saucepan bring three inches of water with ¼ tsp brown sugar to a boil. Add the asparagus and blanch for 2 minutes. Drain asparagus and immediately rinse under cold water to stop cooking process. Set aside.

In a small bowl combine the ingredients for the dressing and blend well. In a large bowl combine the cold chicken, celery, pimiento, asparagus and green onion. Toss well with dressing, cover and chill until ready to serve. Serve topped with fresh chopped basil.

Curried Chicken Salad

Serves 6 to 8

4 chicken breasts, boneless, skinless
4 celery ribs, diced
2 red apples, diced
4 green onions, thinly sliced
½ C cranberries, dried
¾ C cashews, toasted and roughly
   chopped
salt and pepper to taste

Dressing:
¼ C mango chutney, (hot or mild)
¾ C mayonnaise
1 tsp curry powder

Preheat oven to 350 degrees.

Place chicken breasts in roasting pan and bake about 30 to 35 minutes, until juices run clear when pierced. Cool chicken and cut into rough chunks (about ¾ inch square).

Combine dressing ingredients in a small bowl, mix well and set aside. In a large bowl combine chicken, celery, apples, green onions, cranberries, and nuts. Add the dressing, mixing well. Add salt and pepper to taste.

You may serve this salad on top of greens, or as a sandwich filling, perhaps with croissants.

I grew up in a culture that emphasized hospitality and manners, but it was manners with an edge and hospitality that could beggar your soul. As a result, I learned to be wonderful at taking care of others, but backed away from anyone who dared to try to take care of me. So when I came to Hedgebrook, it was almost impossible for me to be comfortable with people who were determined to make my work easier, to serve me wonderful food and encourage me in every way possible to relax and focus on my writing. The first night there, I went back from dinner and sat in the dark almost weeping. Getting used to that determined radical hospitality was one of the hardest things I have done in years—and one of the best. Who would guess that something so simple and basic could be so revolutionary?

—Dorothy Allison

FOUR: FARMHOUSE DINNER

MAIN COURSES

Cioppino

79

Grilled Salmon with Asian Cilantro Sauce

80

Grilled Salmon with Fennel Cucumber Relish

81

Sicilian Snapper

84

Cauliflower Mac and Cheese

85

Roast Chicken

87

Grilled Portabella Mushroom Burgers

90

Turkey Burgers

91

Vietnamese Noodle Salad Bowls

93

Vegetarian Enchiladas

95

Cioppino

Serves 6 to 8

1½ lbs Penn Cove mussels, scrubbed,
  debearded
1½ lbs manila clams, scrubbed
½ lb scallops
1 lb uncooked large shrimp, peeled,
  deveined
1 lb firm white fish (halibut, snapper,
  tilapia) cut into 2 inch chunks
3 T olive oil
1 large onion, chopped
1 fennel bulb, stemmed, cored,
  quartered, sliced
3 cloves garlic, minced
¼ C parsley, chopped, divided
1 can (28 oz) diced, fire roasted tomatoes
2 C dry white wine
8 C clam juice
⅓ C tomato paste
1 T dry basil
1 T dry oregano
½ tsp red pepper flakes, more to taste
2 bay leaves
¼ C Pernod liqueur
salt and pepper to taste
½ C fresh basil, chopped

In a large (6 to 8 qt) heavy pan, over medium heat, add olive oil, stir in onion, garlic, fennel and 2 tablespoons of parsley. Saute until onion is translucent, 8 to 10 minutes. Add tomatoes (including juice), white wine, clam juice, tomato paste, basil, oregano, red pepper flakes, bay leaves and Pernod, stir well. Increase heat and bring to a low boil. Cover, reduce heat to low and simmer for 20 more minutes until flavors are well blended.

Add clams and mussels to the cooking sauce, increase temperature to keep pot at a simmer. Cover and cook until clams and mussels begin to open, about 5 minutes. Stir in scallops, shrimp and fish. Continue to simmer gently until the seafood is just cooked through and the clams and mussels are completely open, about 5 minutes longer. Discard any clams and mussels that do not open. Stir gently, season with salt and pepper to taste.

Ladle into wide bowls and top with remaining parsley and fresh basil. Serve with a nice crusty bread.

Grilled Salmon with Asian Cilantro Sauce

Serves 6 to 8

1 salmon filet, about 1½ to 2 lbs

Marinade:
1 T light soy sauce
1 T dry sherry
1 T sesame oil
1 T ginger, minced

Sauce:
I T ginger, minced
2 garlic cloves, minced
3 T lemon juice
2 T rice vinegar
2 T light soy sauce
1 T sugar
1 T sweet Thai chili sauce (Nuoe cham ga)
½ tsp Sichuan peppercorns, crushed
¼ tsp black pepper
1 T peanut oil
2 T green onions, minced
2 T cilantro, minced
1 T cornstarch
1 T water

In a small bowl mix light soy sauce, dry sherry, sesame oil and minced ginger. Place salmon on a cookie sheet lined in foil (skin side down). Cover with marinade, allow to sit at least 20 minutes (up to 2 hours).

For the sauce, combine ginger and garlic, set aside. In a small bowl, mix together lemon juice, vinegar, soy sauce, sugar, sweet chili sauce, Sichuan pepper and black pepper, set aside. Combine cornstarch with an equal amount of cold water and set aside.

Place a 10 inch sauté pan over medium heat, add peanut oil. When hot add ginger and garlic, sauté for about 30 seconds. Add the lemon juice mixture. Bring to a very low boil, stir in green onions and cilantro. While stirring slowly add as much of the cornstarch mixture as needed to thicken the sauce. Remove from heat and set sauce aside.

Grill or broil salmon for 6 to 8 minutes. Salmon should flake on the surface and remain translucent in the center. Remember salmon will continue to cook after it has been removed from the heat. Place salmon on a serving platter and cover with sauce.

Grilled Salmon with Fennel Cucumber Relish

For Brine:

4 cups water

1 C packed light brown sugar

½ C kosher salt

¼ C granulated sugar

½ C chopped fresh dill

1 salmon filet, about 1½ to 2 lbs

For Relish:

1 lb fennel, stalks discarded and bulb,
    finely chopped

1 lb seedless cucumbers, halved
    lengthwise, cored, and cut into
    ¼-inch dice

6 T cider vinegar, or to taste

2 T shallot, finely chopped

1½ T fresh dill, chopped

1½ T vegetable oil

1 T sugar

¼ tsp salt, or to taste

Bring water, brown sugar, salt, and granulated sugar to a boil in a pot, stirring until sugar is dissolved. Transfer brine to a heat-proof baking dish, then stir in dill and cool. (Brine, without dill, can be made 1 day ahead and kept, covered, at room temperature.)

If you like to eat the skin of the salmon, scale the filets and remove pin bones with tweezers or needle nose pliers. Brine salmon, skin side up, in brine in baking dish, chilled for 1 hour. Do not turn salmon and do not brine for longer than 1 hour.

Prepare grill for cooking.

In a bowl, stir together all relish ingredients and let stand at least 15 minutes. Relish can be made 1 day ahead (though color will not be quite as bright) and chilled, covered. Bring to room temperature before serving.

Remove salmon from brine and pat dry, discard brine. Grill salmon, starting with skin sides up and turning over once, until just cooked through and skin is crisp, about 8 minutes total. Salmon should flake on the surface and remain translucent in the center. Remember salmon will continue to cook after it has been removed from the grill. Serve on a platter with relish on the side.

A Shared Culture

Even before my stay at Hedgebrook, I'd heard about the nightly dinners at the Farmhouse; words like nutritious, organic, and abundant rang through the air. So it was especially comforting to discover that the roots of my Asian upbringing were also so alive each night in the Hedgebrook kitchen. I grew up in the Chinese culture, where food wasn't simply a means of nourishment for the body; food revolved around every aspect of life, taking on new meanings of its own. Tangerines and oranges symbolized "luck" and "wealth," noodles inspired a "long life," pork conjured up "strength," while mixed vegetables meant "family harmony." From the time I was a young girl, food represented growth and love and strength for me. At Hedgebrook, each meal prepared by chefs Denise and Julie was made with the same care and respect and harmony as we gathered around the table each evening.

The Chinese also believe in the Yin and Yang of each prepared dish. The Yin foods reduce the hotness and dryness in the body, while the Yang foods relieve the coldness and dampness. That perfect balance of yin and yang was achieved each evening in the farmhouse. Growing up, happiness in the Chinese culture was a shared event, the simple act of enjoying a good meal with family and friends. In the Hedgebrook culture, it also occurred nightly, nourishing not just the body but the soul.

—Gail Tsukiyama

Sicilian Snapper

Serves 6 to 8

6 to 8 snapper, true cod or tilapia
  filets, cut into serving size pieces
2 to 3 T olive oil
6 to 8 roma tomatoes, quartered
3 to 4 garlic cloves, cut into thin slivers
1 T capers
½ tsp fresh rosemary, chopped
red pepper flakes to taste

Preheat oven to 400 degrees.

Coat the bottom of a large baking dish with olive oil.
(Use a large enough dish to hold the pieces of fish in
one layer.) Scatter the roma tomato quarters, garlic
slivers, capers, rosemary and red pepper flakes in the
bottom of the baking dish. Lay the filets of fish on top
of the tomatoes and drizzle with a little more olive oil.
Bake for 30 minutes, basting every 10 minutes. If fish is
drying out, cover with foil and continue to bake until
fish is done (fish should flake when pulled with a fork in
the center of the filet).

Cauliflower Mac and Cheese

Serves 8 to 10

1 large head cauliflower
1 lb penne pasta
8 T butter, divided
2 T flour
½ C milk
2 C half and half
1 pinch red pepper flakes to taste
1 pinch black pepper to taste
1 pinch ground nutmeg
1 T dry sherry
8 oz Gruyere cheese, grated
8 oz fontina cheese, grated
16 oz sharp cheddar cheese, grated,
    divided
½ C panko (Japanese bread crumbs)
smoked paprika

Preheat oven to 350 degree. Butter a 9 x 13 inch glass baking dish with 1 tablespoon of butter and set aside. Clean and core cauliflower, dividing it into florets. Steam cauliflower until florets begin to soften and can be pierced with a knife. Do not allow cauliflower to overcook and become mushy. Remove from heat, run under cold water, drain and set aside.

Bring medium saucepan of water to boil and add penne pasta. Boil about 8 to 10 minutes. Pasta should be al dente. Remove from heat, run under cold water, drain and set aside.

Place a large heavy saucepan over medium heat, add 4 tablespoons of butter. When butter melts, whisk in flour, continuing to stir as flour cooks a minute or two. Add milk, stirring constantly to avoid lumps. When the sauce is smooth add half and half and continue to stir. Add red pepper, black pepper, nutmeg and sherry, stirring well. Add the three cheeses, reserving ½ C of sharp cheddar for later use. Mix well until all of the cheese has melted and the sauce is consistently smooth. Remove from heat.

Add pasta and cauliflower to the pot of cheese sauce; stir until well mixed. Pour into prepared baking dish. Evenly sprinkle top of baking dish with reserved ½ C of cheddar cheese. Cover with panko and dot with remaining butter. Sprinkle with smoked paprika.

Bake for 40 to 45 minutes, until bubbling and slightly brown on top. Let rest for 10 minutes before serving.

Roast Chicken with Carrots

Serves 6 to 8

1 whole chicken (4 to 5 lbs), rinsed
   (make sure cavity is clean)
1 lemon, zested
10 sprigs of fresh thyme, divided
3 to 4 cloves garlic
1½ tsp kosher salt, divided
1 tsp pepper, divided
2 T butter, softened (or olive oil)
2 onions, cut in wedges
4 carrots, cut into 1 to 2-inch chunks

Preheat oven to 350 degrees.

Rinse chicken and pat dry with paper towels. Zest the lemon and set zest aside. Cut the zested lemon into 6 wedges, and place inside the chicken cavity along with 4 sprigs of thyme.

Mince garlic, and mix with 1 tsp kosher salt. Remove leaves from 6 stems of thyme, and mix with the garlic, along with the lemon zest. Using your fingers or the end of a wooden spoon, separate the chicken skin from the breasts, starting at the neck. Using fingers, insert paste under the skin, working it across the breast.

Rub the whole chicken with butter (or olive oil). Sprinkle all sides with remaining salt and pepper. Place a roasting rack in your roasting pan, and scatter onions and carrots around the edges. Place chicken breast-side-down in roasting pan.

Roast chicken in preheated oven for 20 minutes. Rotate bird on its side, and roast another 20 minutes. Rotate bird to the opposite side and roast for 20 more minutes. Place chicken breast-side-up for the remaining 30 to 40 minutes. When juices run clear when cut into between the leg and thigh, the bird is done. (Total cooking time will be 1 hour 30 minutes to 1 hour 40 minutes.) Remove from oven and tent with foil; let rest for 10 minutes. Skim fat off pan juices and set aside.

Plate chicken with carrots and onions scattered around, pour juices over chicken and veggies, and serve.

You push through the screen door of the farmhouse. You hear other writers talking and laughing inside; you see their shoes lined up in pairs beneath the bench in the foyer. You greet the chef—Denise or Ann or maybe some other lovely person. Another writer comes in behind you, and you know why she's nearly but not quite late—she just couldn't bring herself to get up from her desk. Dinner is ready, and you serve yourself, spooning the food from bright bowls. There's so much of it! It seems more colorful, more delicious-smelling, somehow *foodier* than other, ordinary food. You find your spot on one of the benches flanking the table. Maybe you're looking across the low fields to Useless Bay. Maybe you're facing away from the view, looking across the table at the faces of the other writers. Their faces seem like plenty of view, really. When everyone's seated, there is inevitably a moment of silence as you all consider what you've been given. And then anything can happen. There's philosophy and gossip and politics and craft talk and silliness. There are novels and children and memoirs and lovers and poems and mothers. There's wine, sometimes, and tea and coffee. Now you're pulling snacks from the shelves because, true, you just ate dinner but you need more sustenance. You've been sitting here way longer than you intended. You could stay here forever. You belong here, in this place where nothing is off the table.

—Claire Dederer

Grilled Portabella Mushroom Burgers with Cilantro Aioli

Makes 6 burgers

6 onion buns
butter or olive oil
6 thin slices red onion
2 small ripe avocados, pitted, peeled
   and sliced
Cilantro Aioli
Grilled Portabella Mushrooms

Cilantro Aioli:
1½ C cilantro, sprigs and leaves
2 to 4 cloves garlic, to taste
½ C mayonnaise
1 T lemon juice

Grilled Portabella Mushrooms:
6 portabella mushrooms caps,
   4-6 inches across
¼ C Mirin (Japanese sweet cooking
   rice wine)
2 T soy sauce
2 T water
1 tsp sesame oil

Cilantro Aioli: Place cilantro and garlic in food processor, whirl until coarsely chopped. Add mayonnaise and lemon juice; process until smooth. Taste and adjust flavor. Set aside.

Grilled Portabella Mushrooms: Ignite briquettes or preheat gas or electric grill. Cut stems from mushrooms close to caps and discard. Gently rub mushroom caps clean with a towel. In a small bowl, combine remaining ingredients to make basting sauce.

When coals are covered with a solid layer of ash (medium to medium-hot coals), scatter in a solid even layer or set gas or electric grill on medium to medium-high.

Brush both sides of mushrooms with basting sauce. Set stemmed side down on grill, cook 3 to 4 minutes. Baste and turn over, grill until tops are nicely browned, 2 to 4 minutes. Baste gills generously and turn over again and cook, basting often, until caps are tender when pressed, 4 to 6 minutes more (8 to 12 minutes total).

Lightly butter cut sides of buns; grill or broil until lightly toasted. Lay bottom half of each bun on a plate. Top with onion then avocado slices. Spoon 1½ tablespoons of aioli on each burger, then top with mushrooms and bun tops.

Turkey Burgers

Serves 8

¼ C green onion, thinly sliced
½ C celery, finely chopped
3 tart apples, peeled and diced small
2 T canola oil
4 pounds ground turkey breast
1 T salt
1 T pepper
2 tsp chipotle tabasco
1 lemon, juice and zest
½ bunch parsley, finely chopped
¼ C mango chutney, puréed

Sauté green onion, celery and apple in canola oil until soft. Remove from heat and allow to cool.

In a large mixing bowl combine turkey with sautéed ingredients, salt, pepper, tabasco, lemon juice and zest, parsley and chutney. Shape into eight burgers. Place on baking sheet, cover with wax paper and refrigerate for at least 2 hours.

Cook on a preheated, lightly oiled grill. Grill for about 7 minutes on each side, over medium heat, until meat is thoroughly cooked. Let sit 5 minutes before serving. You can also pan fry these burgers in a non-stick oiled skillet.

Serve with condiments of your choice on toasted buns.

Vietnamese Noodle Salad Bowls

Serves 4 (using large 8 inch bowls)

Choose to marinate one of the following:
- 24 medium to large shrimp, cleaned
- 4 chicken breasts, boned, skinned and cut into 1 inch cube
- 14 oz. tofu, cut into ¼ inch slices

Marinade:
4 cloves garlic, minced
2 inch piece of fresh ginger, peeled and minced
2 T Asian fish sauce
2 tsp sesame oil
1 tsp dried, powdered lemon grass
1 tsp curry powder
1 T sweet Thai chili sauce (Nuoe cham ga)

Dressing:
1 tsp minced garlic and ginger (remaining from marinade recipe)
½ C Asian fish sauce
¼ C rice vinegar
¼ C sugar
¼ C sweet Thai chili sauce (Nuoe cham ga)
1¼ C water

(continued on next page)

Marinade: Combine minced garlic and ginger, reserving 1 tsp for the dressing recipe. Mix all marinade ingredients in a medium bowl. Add shrimp, chicken or tofu and set aside for at least one hour.

Dressing: Mix all dressing ingredients together in small sauce pan, bring to low boil and simmer for a few minutes, stirring to make sure sugar is dissolved. Remove from heat and allow to cool.

Salad Bowls: Bring a large pot of water to boil. Add rice noodles to pot and return to boil. Boil noodles about 3 minutes until tender, slightly soft (do not overcook). Drain noodles and rinse with cold water until no longer hot. Set aside.

Starting with four 8-inch serving bowls, place 2 C of salad greens in the bottom of each bowl. Cover the salad greens with a layer of rice noodles (¼ of the noodles in each bowl). Continue placing ¼ of each of the salad bowl ingredients as follows: in a circular movement around the inside lip of the bowl, starting at the top and moving to the right, place a small pile of grated carrots, followed by a small pile of green onion, next bean sprouts, cucumber, basil, peanuts and back to the carrot

(continued on next page)

(continued from previous page)

Salad Bowls:
14 to 16 oz. package of flat rice stick
  noodles (approx. 1/8 inch wide)
8 C mixed salad greens
4 medium carrots, grated
8 green onions, including greens,
  thinly sliced
8 oz. bean sprouts
1 cucumber, peeled, cut in half
  lengthwise, seeded, thinly sliced
1 C chopped basil
1 C roasted shelled peanuts
lime wedges
2 T canola oil
½ C coconut milk

(continued from previous page)

start. Each bowl should look like the spokes of a wheel, small piles all running into the next. Place a lime wedge in the center of each bowl and you are ready to serve. Place a small bowl of dressing to the side of each noodle bowl, to be used as needed.

After the bowls are prepared and ready to go it is time to cook the shrimp, chicken or tofu. You want to wait until just before you are ready to sit down, it takes just a few minutes and you want it to be hot and not over cooked. Heat 2 tablespoons of canola in a large skillet, add the shrimp, chicken, or tofu. Stir to keep it from sticking to the pan. After a few minutes, test a piece of chicken or shrimp to see if it is done, the tofu should be slightly brown. Add coconut milk scraping the bottom of the pan to get all the goodies. Serve in a separate dish which can be passed around the table and added to the top of the noodle bowls.

Vegetarian Enchiladas

Serves 6 to 8

Filling:
2 C cactus, drained, rinsed, roughly
   chopped (jar)
2 pasilla chilies, charred, peeled,
   seeded and chopped
10 green onions, thinly sliced, divided
1 C cooked chard, drained and chopped

Sauce:
⅓ C canola oil
⅓ C flour
1 quart chicken broth
¼ tsp oregano
¼ tsp ground cumin
4 T pasilla chili powder
2 T California chili powder
1 T New Mexico chili powder

Assembly:
8 corn tortillas
canola oil for frying tortillas
3 C pepper jack cheese, grated
1 C cotija cheese, grated
16 black olives, pitted

In a medium size bowl combine cactus, chilies, 6 green onions and chard. Set aside.

Mix oil and flour together in the bottom of a heavy saucepan. Put on medium to high heat and cook for 5 minutes, stirring constantly to dissolve any lumps. Add broth and whisk vigorously until mixture is well blended. Add oregano, cumin and chili powders. Stir well and continue to cook at a low boil for 5 minutes. Remove from heat and set aside.

Preheat oven to 350 degrees. Cover the bottom of a 9 x 13 inch baking pan with a thin layer of the enchilada sauce and set aside until ready to assemble filled tortillas.

Place ¼ inch of canola oil in a small sauté pan. Heat the oil, frying one tortilla at a time, turning once for a total of 15 seconds per side. Immediately immerse the tortilla in the enchilada sauce, coating each side and stack in baking pan until ready to assemble.

Moisten the filling with a ladle or two of sauce. To form the enchiladas put 1/3 cup filling in the center of each tortilla, top with 1/3 C grated cheese and 2 black pitted olives. Roll up and place side by side in baking dish with the seam side down. (Eight filled tortillas should fit in two rows of 4 in the 9 x 13 inch baking dish.) Ladle more sauce over the enchiladas until covered. Sprinkle top with remaining cheese and green onions.

Bake for 30 minutes until sauce is bubbling and enchiladas are heated through.

SIDES

Zucchini Fritters

99

Curried Cauliflower and Potatoes

100

Fennel Gratin

101

Braised Brussels Sprouts with Pancetta

103

Parsnips and Carrots

105

Seaweed Salad

108

Sweet Potato Fries with Yogurt Lime Sauce

109

Zucchini Fritters

Serves 6 to 8

1 lb zucchini, grated
2 tsp coarse salt
4 scallions, chopped
¼ C dill, minced fine
½ C mint, minced fine
4 eggs, lightly beaten
¾ C pecorino romano cheese, grated
6 T flour
2 to 3 T olive oil (for griddle)

Grate zucchini using a large hole grater or food processor. Place grated zucchini in a large bowl. Mix in salt. Let stand at least 30 minutes. Drain well, squeeze water from zucchini and place zucchini in a clean bowl with scallions, dill, mint, beaten eggs, cheese and flour. Mix together well.

Heat 2 to 3 tablespoons of olive oil on a griddle or a large fry pan over medium heat. Use a quarter cup measure to scoop up zucchini mixture to form pancakes on the griddle or fry pan. Cook on one side until pancakes start to brown. Flip the pancakes and cook until they are firm and nicely browned, about 3 to 4 minutes per side.

Curried Cauliflower and Potatoes

Serves 6 to 8

1-inch piece ginger, peeled and
   julienned
1 tsp cumin seeds
½ tsp black mustard seeds
4 T ghee (butter or canola oil)
3 medium potatoes, sliced into wedges
1 head cauliflower, broken into
   flowerette (similar in size to
   potato pieces)
3 tomatoes, coarsely chopped
1 tsp tumeric
2 tsp ground coriander
1 tsp jaggery (or brown sugar)
1½ tsp salt
3 T parsley or cilantro, chopped

Combine ginger, cumin seeds and mustard seeds in a small bowl, set aside. In a medium to large pot, melt ghee over medium heat. Add the combined ginger and seed mixture. Cook, until seeds pop and sputter. Add potatoes and cauliflower. Cook, stirring, for 5 minutes. Add tomatoes, tumeric, coriander, jaggery and salt. Lower heat and cook covered for another 20 minutes or until vegetables are tender.

Sprinkle with parsley or cilantro before serving.

Fennel Gratin

Serves 8 to 10

3 T olive oil
3 C leeks, chopped (white and pale
  green parts only, about 4 stalks)
3 fennel bulbs, trimmed, cored and
  thinly sliced (reserve fronds)
2 lbs yellow or red potatoes, peeled
  and thinly sliced
1½ C pecorino romano (or parmesan)
1½ C chicken stock
1 C heavy cream
salt and pepper to taste

Preheat oven to 350 degrees.

Butter a 13 x 9 x 2 inch glass baking dish, and set aside.

Place a large skillet over medium heat, add olive oil and leeks. Cook until tender, stirring occasionally, about 10 to 15 minutes. Remove from heat.

Chop ½ C of the reserved fronds and set aside, discard the remaining fronds. In the bottom of the buttered baking dish arrange half of the fennel slices; sprinkle with ¼ C of the chopped fennel fronds, salt and pepper. Next, in a single layer, place half of the potatoes and cover evenly with half of the leek mixture. Sprinkle again with salt and pepper. Cover with half of the grated cheese. Repeat layering in this order, one more time, finishing off the above ingredients.

Mix the chicken stock and cream together in a small bowl and pour slowly over the gratin. Bake uncovered until vegetables are tender and a golden brown, about 1 hour to 1 hour 15 minutes.

Braised Brussels Sprouts with Pancetta

Serves 6

3 oz pancetta, chopped
1 T butter
1 T olive oil
4 shallots, thinly sliced
1 large clove garlic, minced
½ C chicken stock (more if needed)
1 bay leaf
1 sprig thyme, leaves only
6 sprigs parsley, chopped
3 T dry sherry
¼ tsp salt
pinch of black pepper
1 pound Brussels sprouts

Broil thinly sliced pancetta on foil-lined baking sheet for 1 minute or until crisp. Roughly chop and set aside.

In a large sauté pan add butter, oil and shallots. Sauté until shallots begin to brown. Add garlic and cook another minute longer. Add Brussels sprouts and lightly brown.

Add stock, bay leaf, thyme, half of the parsley, sherry, salt, and pepper. Bring to a simmer, cover and cook until Brussels sprouts become tender, just a few minutes.

Remove from heat, sprinkle with remaining parsley and pancetta. Serve warm.

Parsnips and Carrots

Serves 6 to 8

2 T olive oil
1 lb carrots (about 4), peeled, cut into
   3 x ½ inch lengths
1 lb parsnips, peeled, cored and cut
   into similar size pieces as the carrots
coarse kosher salt to taste
pepper to taste
2 T butter
1 T fresh rosemary, chopped
1½ T honey or agave syrup

Heat oil in a large skillet over medium-high heat. Add carrots and sauté for 2 minutes. Add the parsnips. (The carrots take a little longer to cook than parsnips.) Sprinkle with coarse kosher salt and pepper. Sauté until vegetables start to brown at edges and are cooked through, about 12 minutes. You can do this part ahead of time and wait until just before serving to add butter, rosemary and honey to the vegetables. Toss in pan and heat through until vegetables are glazed, about 5 minutes more. Season to taste with salt and pepper.

It was dinner time, thank God, late May. There were two beautiful women in the kitchen, the cook and her friend. The two of them had been out foraging on the beach for seaweed. Walking along, as I see it, maybe picking up the ribbons in their hands, or on a long stick, and maybe a dog was running around too. We do not, as a rule, eat seaweed where I live, in Wisconsin. But there, in the bucket, were the goods, the gift from the sea. The fact of it, dark green, glittery, made us feel as if we were continuing on in the fairytale of our lives, coming from our Hobbityhuts to see what had been hunted and gathered, the freshness of the island being offered up. We sat down and ate, and were fortified.

—Jane Hamilton

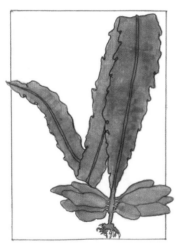  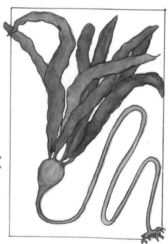

Alaria marginata   Sargassum muticum   Nereocystis luetkeana
(Wing Kelp)   (Wireweed)   (Bull Kelp)

Seaweed Salad (Sunomono)

Serves 6

1 C fresh seaweed, blanched
  Wing Kelp (Alaria marginata)
  Bull Kelp leaf (Nereocystis
  leutkeana)
¾ C Bull Kelp stipe, blanched
½ C Wireweed (Sargassum muticum)
2 large English cucumbers, split
  lengthwise and sliced thin into
  half moons
2 scallions, sliced thin on the diagonal

Marinade:
⅛ C seasoned rice vinegar
2 T Mirin sweet cooking rice wine
1 tsp toasted sesame oil
1 tsp sesame oil with hot chili peppers
2 tsp fresh ginger root, finely grated

1 T whole sesame seeds, toasted
salt to taste

Seaweed collected from Double Bluff and Ebey's Landing when the tides and currents give up their delectable bounty to the happy forager.

Cut freshly harvested Wing Kelp and Bull Kelp blades/leaves into thin ¼ inch strips, a few inches long or longer (like pasta) if you prefer. Cut the stipe of the Bull Kelp crosswise into thin rings, on a diagonal. Blanch by placing seaweeds in a strainer and dipping into just-boiled water 5 to 10 seconds, just until they turn bright green. Run under cold water, drain well, and place in salad serving bowl.

Break fresh raw Wireweed into small pieces and toss together with blanched seaweeds, sliced cucumber and scallions.

Mix all marinade ingredients together in a small bowl and pour over seaweed salad and toss well. Sprinkle with toasted sesame seeds. Add salt to taste.

Sweet Potato Fries with Yogurt Lime Dipping Sauce

Serves 6 to 8

4 medium size sweet potatoes or
   yams, unpeeled
½ C olive oil
2 tsp salt

Yogurt Lime Dipping Sauce:
⅓ C yogurt or sour cream
1 tsp lime zest
1 T lime juice
½ tsp minced garlic
salt to taste

Seasoning Salt:
2 tsp kosher salt
1 tsp ground cinnamon
1 tsp sugar
½ tsp ground cumin
½ tsp ground coriander
¼ tsp paprika

Yogurt Lime Dipping Sauce: Mix all ingredients for the dipping sauce together in a small bowl, chill and set aside.

Preheat oven to 450 degrees.

Wash potatoes and let dry. Leave the peel on and cut the potato on the diagonal into 3/8 inch slices. Cut each slice into 3/8 inch wide sticks. You should end up with a pile of fries all about 2 inches in length. Toss fries in a large bowl with the olive oil and sprinkle with salt. Spread the fries out in a single layer, on a large rimmed baking sheet. Bake in a hot oven for 15 to 20 minutes. Flip the fries with a spatula and return to oven and bake another 10 minutes, once more if necessary, or until fries are nicely brown on the edges. (These fries are never super crispy.)

Seasoning Salt: In a small bowl, mix together all the ingredients in the seasoning salt recipe. As soon as the fries come out of the oven and are still hot, sprinkle them with the seasoning salt.

Serve immediately with Yogurt Lime Dipping Sauce.

FIVE: EVENTS

APPETIZERS

Asparagus Gruyere Tart

Makes 16 pieces

Flour, for work surface
1 sheet frozen puff pastry, thawed
  according to package instructions
2 C Gruyere cheese, shredded
1½ lbs thin or medium thick asparagus,
  rinsed and thoroughly dried
1 T olive oil
salt and pepper to taste

Preheat oven to 400 degrees.

Roll the puff pastry into a 16 x 10-inch rectangle on a floured surface. Transfer pastry onto a baking sheet lined with parchment. Trim uneven edges. With a sharp knife, lightly score pastry dough 1 inch in from the edges to mark a rectangle. DO NOT CUT ALL THE WAY THROUGH THE PASTRY. Using a fork, pierce dough inside the markings at ½ inch intervals. This will make the edges rise up and form a border because they are not pricked. Bake until barely golden, about 5 minutes.

Remove pastry shell from oven. (You may need to press down inner center so it's flat.) Sprinkle the center rectangle with Gruyere cheese. Trim the bottoms of the asparagus spears to fit crosswise inside the tart shell; arrange in a single layer over Gruyere, alternating ends and tips. Brush with oil, and season with salt and pepper. Bake until spears are tender, 15 to 20 minutes. Put tinfoil over edges of pastry for the first 10 minutes, then remove to continue baking.

Remove from oven, transfer pastry to a rack and cool slightly before cutting into serving size pieces. Serve hot or at room temperature.

In Waterfall Cottage, I began weaving an immigrant woman's story about motherhood and its accompanying landmines of the heart. I had no experience with pregnancy at the time, nor had I done much creative writing. Hedgebrook in effect midwifed my birth as a writer.

After my first novel, *Aria*, was published, I had the mental and psychic space to give birth to another baby—this time, a human one. When I first learned I was pregnant, I immediately wanted to visit Hedgebrook. I walked the land, rubbed my belly against an old-growth cedar, and whispered my good news in Nancy Nordhoff's ear.

My second maternal instinct was to breathe in the sights and smells of the Middle East. I settled on my adopted country of Turkey, where my cravings had me feasting on baklava, künefe (filo dough stuffed with cheese and bathed in a sweet syrup), rosewater lokum (Turkish delight), dried figs, apricots and hazelnuts, and aromatic sage, fennel, and rosehip teas.

When my daughter was a month old, I had the great honor of marking her arrival with a tree planting at Hedgebrook. Friends, writers, and staff gathered around a pomegranate-colored Japanese maple between Waterfall and Meadow House, facing a Cherokee dogwood honoring Wilma Mankiller, and blessed my daughter Kiana (whose name means "nature" in Persian, "moon goddess" in Hawaiian, and "garden of the gods" in the Suquamish language). With poetry linked to the earth and toasts to love, Kiana was anointed with Hedgebrook soil and touched her first tree. We celebrated with a feast in the Longhouse. My mother sent Persian food, which we shared with the delicious offerings of the Hedgebrook chefs.

My globally nomadic spirit had come home and had firmly planted its roots.

—Nassim Assefi

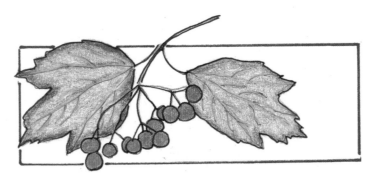

Hummus

Makes 3 cups

2 C chickpeas, drained, (well cooked
   or canned), liquid reserved
2 to 3 cloves garlic
1 tsp salt
2 lemons, juiced, to taste
¾ C tahini
dash of cayenne, or red pepper flakes
black pepper to taste
¼ C minced parsley
smoked paprika

In a food processor add chickpeas, garlic, salt, lemon juice, and tahini. Blend well, slowly adding small amounts of reserved chickpea liquid, as needed, in order to create a very smooth, creamy hummus. Add red and black pepper to taste; mix well.

Place hummus in a serving bowl, top with parsley and sprinkle with smoked paprika. Chill well.

Eggplant Caponata

Serves 6 to 8

2 T salt
1 large eggplant, peeled and cubed
   (½ to ¾ inch cubes)
¼ C olive oil
1 large onion, cut in half lengthwise,
   thinly sliced
4 garlic cloves, minced
1 jalapeño pepper, seeded, diced
2 celery stalks, diced
4 large tomatoes, chopped
½ C olives, pitted and halved
   (green or black)
1 green bell pepper, coarsely chopped
1 red bell pepper, coarsely chopped
1 T parsley, chopped
2 T capers
1 tsp sugar
2 T balsamic vinegar, heated
½ C pine nuts
salt and pepper to taste

Generously salt eggplant and place in nonmetallic strainer to drain. Set aside for about 20 minutes, rinse and dry.

Heat oil in a large pan and sauté eggplant for 3 minutes, remove from pan, set aside. Add onions and garlic, sautéing another few minutes. Add more oil if necessary. Add jalapeño, celery, tomatoes, olives and bell peppers; lower heat and continue cooking for 15 minutes. Add eggplant, parsley, capers to mixture and stir thoroughly. Dissolve sugar in vinegar and add to eggplant mixture. Stir in pine nuts, salt and pepper. Adjust seasonings to taste and cook 5 minutes longer. Serve chilled or at room temperature. (Can be made a day in advance.)

May be served as part of an antipasto platter.

Slow Roasted Tomatoes

Serves 10-12

12 to 14 plum tomatoes (about 2 lbs)
2 T olive oil
¼ tsp salt
2 tsp sugar
2 tsp fresh thyme leaves

Preheat oven to 250 degrees.

Cut the tomatoes lengthwise in half and remove the seeds by poking them out with your fingertip. Toss the tomato halves with the oil, salt, sugar and thyme in a large bowl. Spread the tomatoes in a single layer, cut side up on a baking sheet and bake for about 2 to 3 hours. The tomatoes should be slightly brown on the edges, the skins wrinkled, and have the texture of a soft prune.

Can be made ahead and refrigerated, but bring to room temperature before serving.

Crostini

Makes about 24 small crostini

2 to 3 T olive oil
1 baguette, cut on the diagonal into
   ⅓" slices

Preheat oven to 350 degrees.

Slice the baguette thinly, on the diagonal. Place on a baking sheet and brush with olive oil.

Bake until golden, 10 to 15 minutes.

CROSTINI VARIATIONS

Crostini with Gorgonzola, Walnuts, Figs and Honey

8 oz creamy Gorgonzola, coarsely
crumbled
⅔ C walnuts, toasted and coarsely
chopped
6 ripe figs, thinly sliced
3 T honey, warmed slightly

Preheat oven to 375 degrees.

Mash Gorgonzola and walnuts together in a small bowl.
Spread mixture onto toasted baguette slices and arrange
on a baking sheet. Place in oven and bake for about 8
minutes or until cheese melts.

Transfer to a platter, top each crostini with a few slices
of fig and drizzle with warmed honey.

Crostini with Slow Roasted Tomatoes

24 slow roasted tomatoes
  *see recipe, page 119
24 slices of fresh mozzarella
24 fresh basil leaves
4 T fresh marjoram, chopped

Preheat oven to 350 degrees.

Top each toast with a tomato half, a sprinkle of
marjoram and a slice of mozzarella. Warm crostini in
the oven just until the cheese softens, about 3 minutes.
Transfer crostini to a serving platter and top each with a
basil leaf. Serve immediately.

Gravlax with Grapefruit

Serves 12

Start two to three days before serving.

1 T fennel seeds
1 T white peppercorns
2 tsp black peppercorns
2 tsp coriander seed
⅓ C kosher salt
⅓ C sugar
1 T grated grapefruit zest
2 T fresh grapefruit juice
2 salmon fillets (10 to12 oz each),
  skin on, pin bones removed
1 bunch dill chopped
2 English cucumber (optional)

Coarsely grind fennel seeds, peppercorns, and coriander seeds in spice grinder (or mortar and pestle). Transfer to a bowl, mix with salt, sugar, grapefruit zest and juice.

Place salmon fillets side by side, skin side down, on a large piece of plastic wrap. Scatter the salt mixture over and around the fish. Top one fillet with the dill, then put the other fillet on top, skin-side up. Pat any extra salt mixture all over the fish. Wrap tightly in the plastic wrap and put the fish on a plate. Cover with another plate and put 2 or 3 heavy cans on top to weigh it down.

Refrigerate 2 to 3 days, flipping the salmon daily.

Unwrap salmon, rinse under cold water to remove spices and herbs. Pat dry with paper towels. Slice salmon at an angle as thinly as possible with a sharp knife.

Serve on crostini (see recipe page 119) or English cucumber slices.

Baked Brie

Serves 10 to 12

1 small onion, minced
2 T unsalted butter
½ lb mushrooms, finely chopped
1 T dry sherry
½ tsp nutmeg, freshly grated
salt and pepper to taste
1 package (17 oz) frozen puff pastry
  sheets, thawed according to package
  directions
1 wheel of Brie (14 to 17 oz), chilled
1 large egg

Cook onion in butter over moderate heat in a heavy skillet, until softened. Add mushrooms, sherry, nutmeg, salt and pepper. Sauté over moderately high heat, stirring until the liquid the mushrooms give off has evaporated. Cool and set aside.

On a lightly floured surface, roll out puff pastry dough into a 13-inch square. Using the wheel of Brie as a guide, cut out 1 round the size of the Brie. Cut the wheel of Brie in half horizontally. Roll out remaining sheet of pastry into a 13-inch square. Center bottom half of Brie, cut side up on pastry square and spread mushroom mixture on top. Cover mushroom mixture with remaining half of Brie, cut side down. Without stretching pastry, wrap it snugly up over Brie and trim excess to leave a 1-inch border of pastry on top of Brie. In a small bowl, lightly beat egg and brush onto border. Top Brie with pastry round, pressing edges of dough together gently but firmly to seal. Brush top of pastry with egg, being careful not to let egg drip over edge of pastry (which would prevent it from rising).

Preheat oven to 425 degrees. Chill the pastry-wrapped Brie, uncovered, 30 minutes. (Brie may be made up to this point 1 day ahead and chilled, loosely covered). Place on rimmed cookie sheet or cake pan.

Bake Brie in middle of oven until pastry is puffed and golden, about 20 minutes. Remove from oven, let Brie stand in pan, on a rack, for 15 minutes and transfer with a spatula to a serving plate.

May be served with slices of crusty bread and a fruit conserve.

Ode to a Star Fig

Fig, you are an astral thing.

From how you marquee a tree branch
to your debut on the brunch
tables of my matinee life.

I regret the man in me
that cannot delight in you
without breaking you first.

My crow bar hands pry
your pangaea to continental
drift, and what is all this sea
anemone so packed into you—
all this pink and promise?

Testicle halving to twin vaginas.
Bless you fig, hermaphrodite:
male protecting female, woman
in every man. Utopia
in my mouth: yours
is the sweet of nameless streets
fiber of unanswered inquiry.

How did we get here, and why?
How does sun manage to court all
the planets in that unapologetically
black sky?

—Samantha Thornhill

Figs with Prosciutto

Makes 6 servings

12 large ripe figs
2 sprigs fresh rosemary
2 shallots, thinly sliced
1 bay leaf
2 T extra-virgin olive oil
2 T balsamic vinegar
12 thin slices prosciutto
fresh salad greens arranged on
  6 small individual plates

Preheat oven to 450 degrees.

Place the whole figs in a skillet, just large enough for them to sit up straight against each other. Add the rosemary, shallots, and bay leaf to the skillet, drizzle with the olive oil. Cook over medium heat for 5 minutes, shaking the pan occasionally. Transfer the pan to the oven and bake 10 minutes, shaking the pan twice. Remove the pan from the oven and arrange the figs on the 6 serving plates.

Discard the rosemary and the bay leaf. Whisk the vinegar into the skillet and cook over medium heat until warmed through. Drizzle the figs with the liquid and drape the prosciutto over them. Serve immediately.

Stuffed Mushrooms

Makes 4 dozen

3 T olive oil
2 T butter
48 whole Crimini mushrooms
1 onion, finely chopped
3 celery stalks, finely chopped
1 jalapeño pepper, seeded and finely
   diced
½ bell pepper, seeded and finely
   chopped
2 carrots, grated
½ C parsley, finely chopped
1 lb mild white fish, cut in 1-inch
   chunks
2 C Gruyere cheese (1 lb), grated,
   divided
1 C pecorino romano or paremesan
   cheese, grated
2 eggs, beaten
1 tsp salt
½ tsp pepper
½ tsp smoky paprika
1 C breadcrumbs

Preheat oven to 350 degrees.

Remove stems from mushrooms, mince finely, set aside. Place mushroom caps in two greased 9 x 12 inch glass baking dish.

In a large skillet sauté minced mushroom stems, onions, celery, jalapeño pepper, bell pepper, carrots and parsley in olive oil and butter until partially cooked, about 5 minutes. Nestle fish into veggies to cook, breaking into small pieces, about 2 to 3 minutes. Remove from heat and place mixture in a large bowl. Add 1 cup of Gruyere, 1 cup of pecorino romano or parmesan and beaten eggs. Mix well, add salt, pepper and paprika.

Fill mushroom caps with sautéed mixture, pressing and mounding into each cap. Mix remaining 1 cup of Gruyere with breadcrumbs and spoon onto filled mushroom caps as a topping.

Bake for 45 to 50 minutes.

Smoked Salmon Cheesecake

Serves 18 to 24

Crust:
1½ T butter
½ C breadcrumbs, lightly toasted
¼ C Gruyere cheese, grated
1 tsp fresh dill, chopped (or ¼ tsp dried)

Filling:
1 onion, finely chopped
3 T butter
28 oz cream cheese at room temperature
4 eggs
⅓ C half and half
½ C Gruyere cheese, grated
8 oz smoked salmon, flaked
salt to taste

Preheat oven to 325 degrees.

Crust: Spread butter on the bottom and sides of a 9-inch spring form pan. In a small bowl, combine breadcrumbs, cheese and dill. Sprinkle mixture in pan, making sure to coat the bottom and sides. Refrigerate pan.

Filling: Sauté onions in butter and set aside. In a large bowl, using a mixer, beat cream cheese and eggs until fluffy. Beat in half and half. Carefully fold in Gruyere cheese, salmon, onions and salt to taste.

Pour filling mixture into prepared 9 inch pan and place in a waterbath (Set the 9-inch pan into a larger roasting pan, adding hot water until it is halfway up the sides of the spring form pan.) Bake for 1 hour and 20 minutes, until set.

Turn oven off and let cheesecake cool in the oven with the door ajar, for 1 hour. Transfer cheesecake to cooling rack and serve at room temperature.

ONE-POT

Full Moonssaka

Serves 10 to 12

Roasted Vegetables:
6 zucchini
3 eggplant
10 small to medium potatoes

Lamb Mixture:
3 T olive oil
2 big yellow onions, chopped
5 cloves garlic, minced
2 lbs ground lamb
½ C fresh flat leaf parsley, chopped
2 T fresh marjoram, chopped (2 tsp dried)
2 T fresh oregano, chopped (2 tsp dried)
1 T sage, chopped (1 tsp dried)
2 cans (28 oz each) crushed tomatoes
1 tsp kosher salt
½ tsp pepper

Béchamel Sauce:
8 T butter
8 T flour
4 C milk
2 eggs
1 C parmesan, grated, divided
1 tsp fresh nutmeg, grated
½ tsp salt
¼ tsp white pepper

We were going around the table one night, talking about our comfort foods, and one of the writers said, "Julie, what's your comfort food?" And I said, "Moussaka." And Annie jumped on that and said, "Could we have Moussaka for the Full Moon?"

Preheat the oven to 400 degrees.

Roasted Vegetables: Cut zucchini lengthwise into slices about ½ inch thick. Slice eggplant into ½ inch thick rounds. Put zucchini and eggplant slices on baking sheets lined with paper towels and salt generously to sweat out the water. After about ten minutes, when you see the droplets of water forming, flip them over and do the same to the other side. After another 10 minutes of sweating, dry slices off and place on dry but greased baking sheets.

Peel and slice potatoes into rounds about ¼ inch thick. Place on another greased baking sheet to roast.

Brush or spray olive oil over the tops of all vegetable slices. Roast in oven until slightly brown, about 10 minutes. Flip slices and roast another few minutes. The eggplant and zucchini will be done in less time than the

(continued on next page)

(continued from previous page)

potatoes. The vegetables do not need to be entirely cooked at this point but browning them a little will add flavor to the moussaka. Set aside until ready to assemble.

Lamb Mixture: Add 3 tablespoons of olive oil to a large skillet and sauté chopped onions over medium heat until translucent. Add garlic and cook a few minutes longer. Add ground lamb and stir frequently until it starts to brown. Add all the herbs and crushed tomatoes. Add salt and pepper, bring to a boil, reduce heat and let simmer for 15 to 20 minutes. Set aside until ready to assemble.

Béchamel Sauce: In a 2 quart heavy bottom saucepan melt butter over medium heat. When butter is melted add all the flour at once and whisk vigorously until mixture is smooth and starts to thicken. Do not let this mixture brown or burn. Add 4 cups of warm milk and keep whisking until sauce is smooth and lump free. Turn down the heat and continue whisking. When the béchamel starts to thicken, add beaten eggs, salt and white pepper. Keep whisking and cooking until the sauce coats the back of a spoon. Remove from heat, add ½ cup parmesan, nutmeg and stir well. Set aside until ready to assemble.

Reduce oven to 350 degrees.

Assembly: Oil an 18 x 12 x 3 inch deep baking dish (or use two 9 x 12 inch pans splitting the ingredients between the two pans). First place potato slices in a single layer on the bottom of the baking dish. Spread half the lamb and tomato mixture evenly across the potato layer. The next layer is the eggplant rounds. Spoon the remaining lamb mixture over the eggplant. Add the layer of zucchini slices. Pour the béchamel sauce over the zucchini layer being sure to allow sauce to fill the sides and corners of the pan. Smooth the béchamel on top with a spatula and sprinkle with remaining grated cheese.

Bake for 30 to 45 minutes, until the béchamel topping is starting to brown and the meat and vegetable layers are bubbling hot. Let rest 20 minutes before serving.

Lamb Curry

Serves 10

6 T ghee* or canola oil
1½ T cumin seeds
3 large onions, chopped
14 cloves of garlic, chopped
1 ½ T ginger, finely chopped or grated
3 T ground cumin
3 T ground coriander
1½ tsp tumeric
20 cloves
2 cinnamon sticks (each 3 inches long)
1 tsp ground cayenne pepper
1 T salt
10 ripe tomatoes, chopped
   (about 3 lbs)
2 C plain yogurt, stirred
2 C water
¼ C canola oil
4 lbs leg of lamb, de-boned, fat
trimmed, cut into 1½ inch cubes

In a large heavy stockpot, heat ghee (or canola oil) on medium heat. Add cumin seeds and when they start to pop add the onions and sauté until golden brown. Add garlic and sauté a minute more. Stir in ginger, add cumin, coriander, tumeric, cloves, cinnamon, cayenne and salt. Cook on medium heat, stirring often for 10 minutes. If spices are sticking to the bottom of the pot add another tablespoon of ghee or oil. Add tomatoes and cook another 10 minutes. Stir in yogurt, cook for another minute then add water. Turn heat up and bring to a boil, then remove from heat.

In another large heavy skillet heat ¼ C oil (or enough to cover the bottom of the pan) and sauté the lamb cubes. Keep the heat on medium to high so the meat will sear and start to brown. The lamb does not need to be cooked through at this point, but should be nicely seared to enhance flavor.

Return the curry to medium-low heat, add the seared lamb cubes and cook covered, stirring occasionally, for 2½ hours. If the stew becomes dry add more water, a half cup at a time. Just before serving, remove the cinnamon sticks.

* Ghee is an Indian clarified butter product which can be purchased at a specialty food store.

Italian Chicken Stew

Serves 6 to 8

6 chicken pieces, boned, skinned,
   (thighs and/or breasts)
¼ C flour
½ tsp salt
1 tsp lemon pepper (or black pepper)
3 T olive oil
4 Italian chicken sausages
6 cloves garlic, minced
½ tsp fennel seed
1 large pinch red pepper flakes
2 T capers, drained
1 lemon, zest and juice
¾ C dry white wine
1½ C chicken broth (more if necessary)
1 lb yukon gold potatoes, cut into
   1-inch cubes
1 fennel bulb, cored and chopped
   coarsely
8 to 12 oz thawed frozen artichoke
   hearts, cut into quarters (or canned
   artichoke hearts in water, drained)
½ C parsley, finely chopped
1 C whole green pitted olives

Cut chicken into large pieces (a thigh into 3 pieces). Mix flour, salt and pepper in medium bowl and toss in chicken pieces, a few at a time, making sure each piece is coated. Heat olive oil in a large heavy pot over medium heat. Sauté pieces, one layer at a time, cooking until brown, turning once, 4 to 5 minutes. Transfer to a plate and set aside.

Brown sausage in the same pan adding a little more olive oil if needed. Remove and set aside. When cool enough to handle, cut sausage into 1-inch lengths.

Reduce heat and slightly brown garlic and fennel seed. Add red pepper flakes, capers, and lemon zest, stir about 30 seconds. Add wine and simmer scraping the brown bits from the bottom of the pan. Cook about 2 minutes. Add broth, chicken and sausage, return to a simmer. Add potatoes and fennel, continue to simmer about 10 minutes. Add artichokes and cook until potatoes are done.

Stir in olives, parsley, and lemon juice. Serve hot.

I come from a family who show their affection through cooking and feeding. Because I was born and raised in the States, I have also learned to hug and talk about my feelings, but my inclination is to always cook to show I care. I love Hedgebrook to pieces and am forever grateful and indebted to the vision, dedication, and generous hospitality of the Hedgebrook family.

Pho for Hedgebrook came up in conversation with Vito. I was thrilled for a chance to cook as a small token of my enormous gratitude. Julie so graciously agreed to help (by "help" I mean it would not have been possible without her), and then to really up the ante Vito volunteered the services of the grass-fed, apple-finished Red Angus in the freezer, who was well treated in life and would be well appreciated in death.

I learned how to make pho from my mother. These days whenever I go home, I get additional tips from my aunt. They involve brazenly charring things over open flames, which is a real boon for this rough-and-tumble musician image I'm trying to maintain.

I was so touched to see Hedgebrook folks and their families gathered in the farmhouse, coming back to the jobsite on a Saturday night. To make and share a dish that has such personal roots was sweet and poignant. I was quite fortunate to serve as a sort of bridge from one family to another, and even more fortunate for my membership in both.

—Thao Nguyen

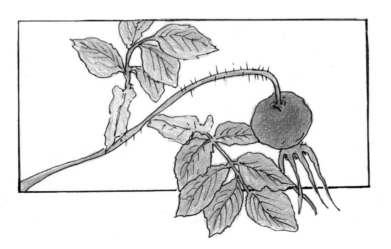

Pho Bo

(continued on next page)

Serves 20

Broth:

10 lbs beef soup bones

4 lbs beef chuck roast, cut into 2 pieces

4 lbs short ribs

8 pieces ginger (each 3 inches long),
  lightly charred *

8 yellow onions, peeled, charred*

1 C fish sauce

¾ C granulated sugar

40 whole star anise, lightly toasted in a
  dry pan

24 whole cloves, lightly toasted in a dry
  pan

8 cinnamon sticks (each 3 inches long)

20 cardamom pods

4 T sea salt

Noodle and Beef Assembly:

4 lbs dried 1/16 inch wide rice sticks **,
  cooked and drained

1½ lbs beef sirloin, slightly frozen, then
  sliced paper-thin across the grain

* **To Char Ginger and Onions:** Cut each piece of ginger in half lengthwise and smash lightly with the flat side of a knife. Hold the piece of ginger with tongs directly over an open flame or place it directly on a medium-hot electric burner. Rotate the ginger and char until the edges are slightly blackened and the ginger is fragrant, about 3 to 4 minutes. Char the onions in the same way. Peel and discard the blackened parts of the skins of the ginger and the onions, then rinse and drain and hold until ready to add to broth.

Broth: In a very large stockpot bring 12 quarts of water to a boil. Place bones, beef chuck and short ribs in a second pot large enough to hold them. Cover them with water, bring to a boil and boil vigorously for 5 minutes. Using tongs, transfer bones and beef to the first pot of boiling water. Discard the water in which the meat was just cooked. (This cleans the bones and meat and reduces the impurities that cloud the broth.) When the water returns to a boil, reduce the heat to a simmer. Skim the surface often to remove any foam and fat. Add the charred ginger and onions, fish sauce and sugar. Simmer until the beef chuck is tender, about 40 minutes. Remove one piece of the chuck and submerge in cool water for 10 minutes to prevent the meat from darkening and drying out. Drain, then cut into thin slices and set aside. Let the other piece of beef chuck continue to cook in the simmering broth.

(continued from previous page)

Garnishes:
2 yellow onions, sliced paper-thin
8 scallions, cut into thin rings
1 C cilantro, chopped
3 lbs bean sprouts
20 sprigs Thai basil
20 Thai bird chilies or 3 Serrano
  chilies, cut into thin rings
4 limes, cut into thin wedges
black pepper, freshly ground

Simmer broth for another 1½ hours. Wrap and tie up the star anise, cloves, cinnamon sticks, and cardamom in a piece of cheesecloth and add to the broth. Let infuse until the broth is fragrant, about 45 minutes more. Remove and discard the spice bag, onions and ginger. Add the salt and continue to simmer, skimming as necessary, until you are ready to assemble the dish. The broth needs to cook for at least 2 hours. The broth will taste salty but will be balanced once the noodles and accompaniments are added. Leave the remaining chuck and bones to simmer in the pot while you assemble the bowls.

**To Cook the Noodles: Rice sticks, or banh pho, are translucent linguini shaped dried noodles sold in Asian markets. For pho, buy the small, 1/16th-inch-wide variety. To prepare them, first soak them in cold water for 30 minutes and drain. Then bring a large pot of water to a rolling boil. When you are ready to serve, place the noodles, one portion at a time, into a sieve and lower it into the boiling water. Using chopsticks or a long spoon, stir so the noodles untangle and cook evenly. Blanch just until they are soft but still chewy, about 10 to 20 seconds. Drain completely and transfer to the preheated bowls. Cook remaining noodles the same way. You may also cook the noodles all at once by adding them directly to the pot of boiling water, just make sure to serve them immediately.

To Serve: Place the cooked noodles in preheated bowls. (If the noodles are not hot, reheat them in a microwave or dip them briefly in boiling water to prevent them from cooling down the soup.) Place a few slices of the beef chuck and raw sirloin on top of the noodles. Bring the broth to a rolling boil and ladle about 2 cups into each bowl. The broth will cook the raw beef instantly. Garnish with yellow onions, scallions and cilantro. Serve immediately, inviting guests to garnish the bowls with the bean sprouts, herbs, chilies, limejuice and black pepper.

Vegetarian Lasagna

Serves 8 to 10

Red Sauce:
2 T olive oil
1 medium yellow onion, diced
4 cloves garlic, finely chopped
1 T basil, dried
1 T oregano, dried
1 T rosemary, dried, crushed
1 T fennel seeds
½ tsp red pepper flakes
1 can (28 oz) whole tomatoes, fire
    roasted
1 jar (25.5 oz) marinara sauce
1 C dry red wine
1 green bell pepper, diced
8 oz mushrooms, sliced

Vegetable Layers:
3 T olive oil
1 large eggplant, peeled, sliced into ½
    inch thick rounds
2 medium zucchini, sliced into ⅓ inch
    thick rounds

(continued on next page)

Red Sauce: In a large heavy bottomed saucepan, sauté onions and garlic in oil over medium heat, stirring occasionally until onions are translucent, about 10 minutes. Add dried herbs, fennel and pepper flakes, stir together. Drain the juice from the canned tomatoes into the cooking mixture and stir. Using your hands break the whole tomatoes into large pieces and add to the pot. Add the marinara sauce, wine, bell pepper and mushrooms, mix well. Cover and keep at a low simmer, stirring occasionally. Simmer a minimum of 2 hours.

Vegetable Layers: Preheat oven to 350 degrees.

Paint eggplant slices with olive oil on both sides. Spread slices on parchment covered cookie sheet and bake for 20 to 25 minutes or until golden brown. Steam zucchini for a few minutes until they begin to soften. Rinse with cold water to halt cooking process and drain. In a medium bowl, stir together steamed greens, egg, nutmeg, ricotta cheese and basil.

Assembly: Using a 9 x 12 inch baking dish (preferably one with tall sides) begin assembling the lasagna. Cover the bottom of the pan with a thin layer of red sauce, cover with a single layer of lasagna noodles and another thin layer of red sauce. Next add the layer of eggplant slices. Cover with half of the provolone slices, a noodle layer and another layer of red sauce. Add a layer of

(continued from previous page)

1 C steamed chard or spinach,
   drained, chopped
1 egg, beaten
¼ tsp nutmeg
1 C ricotta cheese
1 C fresh basil, chopped
1½ lbs provolone cheese, sliced
1 box (9 oz) lasagna noodles,
   ("no boiling required" type)

zucchini and cover with the ricotta mixture. Follow with a noodle layer and another layer of red sauce. The dish is topped off with the remaining sliced provolone (be generous with your two provolone layers).

Before placing the lasagna into the oven, tent the pan with foil by using short wooden skewers to hold the foil above the cheese layer. Place the lasagna pan on a rimmed baking sheet to prevent spilling over into the oven as it cooks.

Bake for 1 hour. Let rest 20 minutes before serving.

SIX: DESSERTS

Applesauce Cake

Serves 12

3 C flour
2 tsp baking soda
1 tsp salt
1½ tsp ground cinnamon
1¼ tsp ground cardamom
1 C (2 sticks) unsalted butter,
    room temperature
2 C packed light-brown sugar
¼ C honey
2 large eggs, room temperature
2 C applesauce
canola oil spray
powdered sugar (optional)

Preheat oven to 350 degrees.

In large bowl, whisk together flour, baking soda, salt, cinnamon and cardamom. Set aside.

In another bowl with an electric mixer, beat butter, brown sugar and honey until light and fluffy, 3 to 4 minutes. Add eggs, one at a time, beating well after each addition. With mixer on low speed, gradually add flour mixture; beat just until combined. Mix in applesauce.

Generously coat 9-inch tube pan with canola oil spray. Spoon batter into pan, smooth top.

Bake 50 to 60 minutes until a toothpick inserted in the middle comes out clean (but slightly wet). Cool in the pan, on a wire rack, for 10 minutes then invert cake onto rack, top-side up. Cool completely.

Dust with powdered sugar before serving, if desired.

Chocolate Ganache Tarts

Makes 6 individual tarts

1 C vanilla wafers, crushed
   (about 22 wafers)
4 T butter, at room temperature
3 oz milk chocolate (33%),
   finely chopped
5 oz dark chocolate (72%),
   finely chopped
1¼ C heavy cream
1 vanilla bean, scraped

Crush cookies in a food processor or in a plastic bag using a rolling pin. Melt the butter in a small saucepan and mix in the crumbs. (All the cookie crumbs should be moist.) Press the crumbs into the bottom of 6 (⅓ C sized) individual ramekins forming a dense crust about ¼ inch thick. (Use a flat-bottomed glass to press the crumbs into the pans very firmly.) Chill the prepared ramekins for one hour.

Place both chocolates in a medium size bowl. In a small saucepan, heat cream with the seeds of 1 large vanilla bean. When this mixture reaches 130 degrees, pour it over the chocolate. Do not stir now. Wait about two minutes to give the chocolate time to melt, then begin to stir slowly in a circular motion until all of the cream and chocolate are blended together.

Pour the ganache into the prepared ramekins. Let sit until the ganache comes to room temperature then refrigerate for at least 2 to 3 hours. Remove tarts from refrigerator 45 minutes before serving. (The tarts are best served at room temperature.)

Top with whipped cream and dust with cocoa powder.

Apple Raspberry Crisp

Serves 10 to 12

Fruit:
6 C apples, peeled and diced
2 T lemon juice
4 C raspberries (previously frozen
   are fine)
½ C sugar
2 T minute tapioca
½ tsp ground cinnamon
½ tsp ground ginger

Topping:
1 C butter, melted
1 C brown sugar
1 C flour
½ tsp baking soda
½ tsp baking powder
1 C nuts, chopped
1½ C rolled oats

For the Fruit: Preheat oven 350.

Place diced apples in a bowl and sprinkle with lemon juice. Add raspberries. Mix sugar, tapioca, cinnamon, and ginger together in a small bowl. Toss with fruit until well coated. Place mixture in a buttered 9 x 12 inch glass baking pan and set aside.

Topping: In a medium bowl mix butter and brown sugar. In a smaller bowl mix flour, baking soda and baking powder. Add flour mixture to butter and sugar mixture, stir well. Add chopped nuts and rolled oats, mix until combined.

Spread topping mixture evenly across the apple raspberry mixture. Tamp down gently.

Bake for about 45 minutes. Crisp is done when fruit is bubbling and topping is golden brown.

I've had all sorts of dinners at Hedgebrook. I've had dinners when I laughed so hard I spilled my wine, dinners of wit, merriment, and raucous singing. I've had sorrowful dinners when someone at the table honored us with a painful history never told before. I've had shy dinners when no one yet knew anyone well enough for any of the above. But throughout, these two things remain constant: the food is always amazing, and the writers at the table are always amazed by it.

Hedgebrook hosts many women like myself who are not used to being cooked for. Such women know how to value a Hedgebrook meal. Like everything else there—the cottages, the solitude and silence, the woods and ponds, beautiful in all seasons and weathers—the food tells us that someone believes our work is important. This often comes to women as a powerful surprise.

Our work, Hedgebrook says, is not just worth any old dinner (which would have already been a great thing to be told.) No, our work is worth rhubarb cake, chocolate shortbread, carrots and raspberries fresh from the garden, jars of dried fruits, nuts, just-picked salads and just-cooked soups. Our work is worth fabulous curries, pastas, and potpies. Our work is worth a meal creatively, thoughtfully, and lovingly prepared. Poems have been written about the figs and grapes, the gardeners and the cooks of Hedgebrook.

Nobody goes to Hedgebrook for the food.

But everyone would stay for it if only they could.

—Karen Joy Fowler

Carrot Cake

Serves 10 to 12

Cake:
1½ C canola oil
2 C sugar
4 eggs
1 tsp salt
1 tsp ground cinnamon
2 C flour
2 tsp baking soda
3 C carrots, finely grated (about 1½ lbs)
1 C almonds, blanched, finely chopped

Cream Cheese Icing:
8 oz cream cheese, softened
4 T butter, melted
2 T vanilla
8 oz powdered sugar

For the Cake: Preheat oven to 325 degrees.

Blend oil and sugar in large bowl with a wooden spoon. Add the eggs, one at a time, beating well after each addition.

In another bowl, sift together salt, cinnamon, flour, and baking soda. Add the sifted ingredients to the egg mixture, and stir until they are thoroughly incorporated. Add carrots and almonds and mix in well.

Grease a 9 x 12 inch cake pan. Pour batter into prepared cake pan and bake for 1¼ hours, or until a toothpick inserted in the center comes out clean (but slightly wet). Remove from oven and place cake on a cooling rack. Leave cake in pan, when cake is completely cool, cover with icing.

For the Icing: With an electric mixer, beat cream cheese until light and fluffy. Gradually add the melted butter and continue beating until completely absorbed. Add the vanilla and sugar, beating well until icing is smooth.

Chipotle Brownies

Makes 9 servings

¼ C flour
2 T unsweetened cocoa powder
1 tsp baking powder
½ tsp ground cinnamon
1 tsp chipotle powder
½ tsp salt
¼ C unsalted butter, cut into
   small pieces
2 oz unsweetened chocolate, chopped
3 oz semisweet chocolate, chopped
3 eggs
¾ C sugar
½ tsp vanilla extract
⅓ C sour cream
4 oz chocolate chunks (⅔ C)

Preheat oven to 325 degrees.

Combine flour, cocoa, baking powder, cinnamon, chipotle powder and salt in a medium bowl and set aside.

Melt butter, unsweetened chocolate and semisweet chocolate in a metal bowl set over a saucepan with one inch of simmering water (or use a double boiler). Remove from heat and stir until smooth.

In the bowl of a stand mixer with a whisk attachment, combine eggs, sugar and vanilla. Whisk on high speed until slightly thickened, about 1 to 2 minutes. Pour in the melted chocolate mixture and whisk on medium for 30 seconds. Add the flour mixture and whisk on low for 30 seconds. Add sour cream and whisk on medium for 30 seconds. Stir in chocolate chunks by hand.

Butter an 8 x 8 inch baking pan and dust with cocoa powder. Pour batter into prepared baking pan. Bake for 35 to 45 minutes, or until a toothpick inserted in the center comes out clean. Cool on wire rack 10 minutes. Cut into serving size squares.

Pear Galette

Serves 6 to 8

Sweet Galette Dough:
Makes 2 crusts

2½ C flour
2 T sugar
½ tsp salt
½ C unsalted butter, chilled, cut into
  small pieces
¼ to ½ C ice water

Poached Pears:
2 C white wine
4 C water
1 C sugar
1 lemon, juice and zest
1 cinnamon stick (3 in)
1 vanilla bean, split
4 pears, peeled (firm but ripe)

Almond Frangipane Filling:
½ C butter
½ C sugar
¾ C almonds, blanched, ground fine
1 large egg
1 tsp pure almond extract
1 T flour

Assembly:
2 T butter, melted
2 T sugar

Dough: In a food processor pulse together flour, sugar and salt. Add chilled butter pieces and process (about 10 seconds) until butter is evenly distributed but still in large visible pieces. Pulse processor while adding small amounts of ice water until dough just holds together. Do not process more than 30 seconds. Turn dough out on a floured surface and squeeze dough with your hands to form two equal disks. Wrap each disk in plastic wrap and refrigerate at least one hour. (Freeze any unused dough well wrapped in plastic; defrost the frozen dough in the fridge for a day before using it.)

Poached Pears: In a large saucepan combine wine, water, sugar, lemon juice and zest, cinnamon stick and vanilla bean. Bring to a boil and cook for 5 minutes. Add pears. Remove from heat and allow pears to cool in the liquid. Once pears are completely cool, quarter the pears, core and slice them into thin equal sized wedges. Set aside until ready to assemble galette. (Poaching liquid can be reserved by freezing for a later use.)

Frangipane Filling: In a medium bowl combine butter and sugar and beat until light and fluffy. Add ground almonds, egg, almond extract, and flour, and beat until smooth.

(continued on next page)

(continued from previous page)

Assembly: Preheat oven to 400 degrees.

Roll the dough into a 13 to 15-inch circle on a piece of floured parchment and transfer dough (on parchment) to a baking sheet. Spread frangipane filling evenly onto center of the dough leaving a 2-inch border. Arrange sliced fruit in concentric circles, overlapping slightly on top of frangipane. Lift edges of dough and fold them inward over the filling, pleating as you go. Brush the border with melted butter and sprinkle the entire galette with sugar. Chill the galette on its baking sheet for at least 30 minutes. Bake for 35 to 45 minutes until crust is nicely browned. Slide galette off parchment and onto a cooling rack. Let cool for about 10 minutes before slicing.

Vanilla Bean Panna Cotta

Serves 8

½ C cold water
2½ tsp Knox gelatin powder
4 C whipping cream
½ C sugar
2 vanilla beans, split open

In a small Pyrex bowl, mix cold water with gelatin powder. Allow to sit 5 minutes or until it becomes completely softened.

Meanwhile, in a large saucepan heat the cream, sugar, and vanilla beans just to a boil, then immediately remove from heat.

In a wide shallow saucepan heat one inch of water to simmer. Place the Pyrex bowl with the gelatin mixture into the simmering water bath. The gelatin will liquefy in about one minute. Using a pot holder, remove bowl from the water bath and stir once to make sure gelatin is liquefied.

Slowly pour the gelatin mixture, while whisking, into the hot cream mixture. Continue whisking for about 3 minutes or until the gelatin is totally integrated into the cream.

Place 8 half-cup size ramekins on a rimmed cookie sheet. Remove the vanilla beans and pour the panna cotta into the ramekins. When cooled to the touch, cover with a piece of parchment paper, refrigerate for a minimum of 5 hours before serving.

Vito's Flourless Chocolate Cake

Serves 8 to 10

12 oz bittersweet chocolate (72%),
  chopped
1½ sticks unsalted butter, cut in
  pieces
6 large eggs, separated
12 T sugar, divided
2 tsp vanilla

Preheat oven to 350 degrees.

Melt chocolate and butter in heavy saucepan. Stir over low heat until smooth.

In a medium bowl, beat egg yolks with 6 tablespoons of sugar until thick and pale. Fold in the chocolate mixture and vanilla.

In a separate bowl, beat egg whites briefly and add 6 tablespoons of sugar. Continue to beat until egg whites are the consistency of heavy cream, but not stiff.

Fold whites into chocolate and egg yolk mixture in three additions.

Butter and line a 9-inch spring form pan with parchment. Pour batter into pan and bake for 50 minutes. Test with a toothpick, which should come out clean when inserted in middle of cake. Cool in pan.

Note: Top of cake will rise in oven and fall upon cooling.

Cheesecake

Serves 8 to 10

24 oz cream cheese
6 eggs, separated
1 C sugar
2 T flour
1 C sour cream
1 tsp lemon juice
1 tsp vanilla

Preheat oven to 325 degrees.

In a medium size bowl beat cream cheese and egg yolks until smooth. Add sugar, flour, sour cream, lemon and vanilla and mix well.

Whip egg whites until stiff peaks form. Gently fold whites into cream cheese mixture, being careful not to overmix.

Line the bottom of a 9-inch spring form pan with parchment. Pour in batter.

Bake for 1 hour and 10 minutes or until center no longer appears soft.

Cool at least 2 hours before serving.

Rhubarb Cake

Serves 8

½ C butter (soft)
1 C sugar
3 large eggs
1½ C unbleached flour
3 tsp baking powder
¼ tsp salt
½ C milk
1 tsp vanilla extract
2½ C rhubarb, sliced ¾ to 1 inch
  pieces (about 4 stalks)
2 T minute tapioca

Preheat oven to 350 degrees.

With an electric mixer in a large bowl, cream butter and sugar until light and fluffy. Add eggs, one at a time, beating well after each addition. In separate bowl sift together flour, baking powder and salt. In separate bowl combine milk and vanilla. Alternate adding wet and dry ingredients to butter mixture and continue to mix well.

In a bowl, mix rhubarb pieces with tapioca and set aside.

Butter and flour a 9 x 9 inch glass baking dish. Spread half the batter into the prepared baking dish. Scatter rhubarb mixture evenly over the batter. (Do not press rhubarb down.) Top with the rest of batter.

Bake 35 to 40 minutes. Test with a toothpick, which should come out clean when inserted in middle of cake.

Variation: Replace rhubarb with 2½ C blueberries or 2½ C raspberries

Lemon Polenta Cake with Rosemary Syrup

Makes 1 loaf

1½ C polenta (corn grits)
½ C flour
1½ tsp baking powder
¼ tsp salt
5 T plain yogurt
5 T vegetable oil
2 lemons, zested
2 T lemon juice
2 C sugar, divided
2 eggs
2 egg whites
1 C water
2 sprigs fresh rosemary

Preheat oven to 350 degrees.

Whisk polenta, flour, baking powder and salt in a medium size bowl and set aside. In a small bowl combine yogurt, oil, lemon zest and juice and stir well. In a large bowl, beat eggs and egg whites with 1 cup of the sugar until well incorporated. Add yogurt mixture and continue to beat until smooth. Fold in dry ingredients and mix until just blended. Do not overmix.

Oil and line a 9-inch loaf pan with parchment paper. Pour batter into pan. Bake 40 to 45 minutes. Test for doneness with a toothpick.

Meanwhile in a small saucepan, combine remaining cup of sugar with 1 cup of water and rosemary. Bring to a boil and simmer for 10 minutes. Cool the syrup completely and strain.

When cake is done, cool on rack for 15 minutes then invert. Remove cake from pan. With a toothpick, prick the cake on all sides and drizzle with half the syrup. Let cake cool completely. Cut cake into slices and serve with more syrup drizzled over each slice if desired.

Her Giant Silence

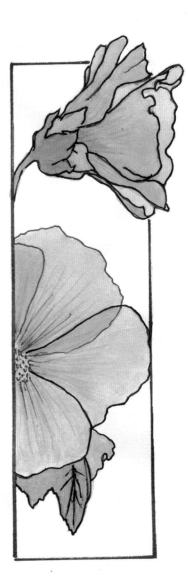

A mother owl behind the woodshed dropped down from the pine
flapped a great silence above me and flew off,
changing her direction four times before disappearing from my sight.
I was stunned by her giant silence.
I walked back to Oak Cabin and lay down.
The kitchen that night was suffused with the smells of creation,
the sweating goddess in her long black apron smiled and stirred,
concentrated and opened the oven door,
taking out a dessert with a French name, filled with raspberries.
The farmer had taught me how to pick nettles and whack
my knees with them to help the arthritis.
But for tonight, I put all stinging cures aside,
I calmed my mind from my torrent of words.
Opened my mouth for the raspberry and cream
Lit a fire,
hummed

—Annie Rachele Lanzillotto

Salted Caramel Ice Cream

Makes 1 quart

1¼ C sugar, divided
2¼ C heavy cream, divided
½ tsp flaky sea salt (such as Maldon)
½ tsp pure vanilla extract
1 C whole milk
3 large eggs

Heat 1 cup sugar in a dry 10-inch skillet over medium heat, stirring with a fork to heat sugar evenly until it starts to melt. Stop stirring but continue to cook the mixture by swirling the skillet occasionally so sugar continues to melt evenly and turns amber. Add 1¼ C cream (mixture will splatter) and cook, stirring, until all of caramel has dissolved. Transfer to a bowl and stir in sea salt and vanilla. Cool to room temperature.

Bring milk, remaining cup of cream and remaining ¼ cup of sugar just to a boil in a small heavy saucepan, stirring occasionally. Lightly whisk eggs in a medium bowl, then add half the milk mixture to the eggs in a slow stream, whisking constantly. Pour back into saucepan and cook over medium heat, stirring constantly with a wooden spoon, until custard coats back of spoon and registers 170 degrees on an instant-read thermometer. DO NOT LET BOIL or mixture will curdle.

Pour custard through a fine mesh sieve into a large bowl, then stir in the cooled caramel.

Chill custard, stirring occasionally, until very cold, 3 to 6 hours. Freeze custard in ice cream maker (it will be quite soft), then transfer to an airtight container and freeze to firm up.

Honey Lavender Ice Cream

Makes 1 quart

2 C heavy cream
1 C half and half
⅔ C honey
2 T dried edible lavender flowers
2 large eggs
⅛ tsp salt

In a 2-quart heavy saucepan bring cream, half and half, honey and lavender to a boil over medium heat, stirring occasionally. Remove pan from heat. Let steep, covered for 30 minutes.

Pour cream mixture through a fine sieve into a bowl and discard the lavender flowers. Return mixture to a clean saucepan and heat over medium heat until hot.

Whisk together eggs and salt in a small bowl and add 1 cup of the hot cream in a slow stream while whisking. Pour egg and cream mixture into remaining hot cream in saucepan and cook over moderate heat, stirring constantly with a wooden spoon until thick enough to coat back of spoon. It will take about 5 minutes. DO NOT LET BOIL or mixture will curdle.

Pour custard through fine mesh sieve into cleaned bowl and cool completely. Chill, covered, until cold, at least 3 hours or overnight.

Freeze custard in ice cream maker. Transfer ice cream to an airtight container and put in freezer to harden.

Raspberry Moscato Sorbet

Makes 1 quart

⅔ C sugar
⅔ C water
2½ C raspberries (frozen are fine)
1 C Moscato late harvest wine or
 Vin Santo*
1½ T fresh lemon juice

In a small heavy saucepan combine sugar and water and bring to a boil, stirring until the sugar is dissolved. Remove from heat and set aside.

In a blender or food processor purée raspberries with the wine and sugar syrup until smooth. Force purée through a fine sieve set over a bowl. Add lemon juice to purée.

Chill mixture until cold. Freeze in an ice cream maker. Transfer to a container, cover and freeze.

* Vin Santo is an Italian dessert wine sold at specialty food stores and liquor stores.

SEVEN: CHEF'S PANTRY

Dijon Balsamic Vinaigrette
175

Buttermilk Dressing
175

Caesar Dressing
177

Blue Cheese Dressing
177

Lemon Vinaigrette
178

Asian Ginger Dressing
178

Cranberry Vinaigrette
179

Honey Mint Vinaigrette
179

For three months during the spring of 2000, swaddled in the shadows of Oak Cottage, I worked on a novel-in-progress that didn't yet have a name. My main character, Binh, was a cook, and I was tracing his journey from the outsized kitchen of the French Governor-General's house in colonial Saigon to the intimate one of Gertrude Stein and Alice B. Toklas in 1920s Paris.

What I was attempting to do on the page—assembling the bare bones of a kitchen and stocking it only with necessities rich in narrative—had a corollary to what I was doing in Oak Cottage. An avid cook, I was used to a well-stocked kitchen, not one that offered only one burner, a frying pan, a pot, a plate, and a mug. Everything present was functional, necessary, and elemental. I took pleasure from the nightly gathering of the few ingredients that would allow me to cook my breakfast the following morning: the eggs, in odd sizes and pastel hues; the chunk of butter; the piece of bread; and the spoonfuls of black pepper and coarse sea salt.

There it was. "Salt," the main word of the eventual title of my novel—*The Book of Salt*—was everywhere in my manuscript, but I couldn't see it. I couldn't appreciate the pervasiveness or significance of salt to Binh or to his story because I had overlooked the role that it played in my and every kitchen. When you stripped away the saffron threads, the bay leaves, the sumac, the cardamom pods, you are left with the grains that are the foundation of every culinary tradition, the element that our bodies crave in order to live, the one ingredient that I knew for certain was present in every kitchen that Binh has ever been in, and thus the constant companion that I could give to my lonesome cook.

—Monique Truong

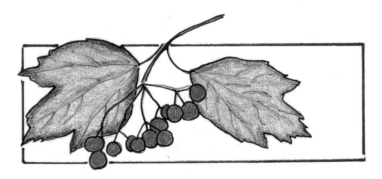

Dijon Balsamic Vinaigrette

Makes 1 cup

1 T Dijon mustard
2 cloves garlic, minced
1/3 C balsamic vinegar
2/3 C extra-virgin olive oil
1/4 tsp salt
1/8 tsp black pepper
1 T fresh herbs, minced or 1 tsp dried

Whisk Dijon mustard, garlic and vinegar in a small bowl. Drizzle olive oil slowly into the bowl while whisking constantly. The dressing should start to emulsify.

Add salt, pepper and herbs of your choice, to taste.

Buttermilk Dressing

Makes 1 cup

½ C sour cream
½ C buttermilk
1 T chives or green onions, minced
½ tsp garlic, finely chopped
2 T fresh parsley, minced
½ tsp salt
¼ tsp pepper
⅛ tsp hot pepper sauce (optional)

In a small food processor or blender, combine all ingredients and blend until smooth. Transfer to a covered bowl or jar and refrigerate for at least 1 hour.

Will keep refrigerated for up to 3 days.

Caesar Dressing

Makes 1 cup

½ C olive oil
2 to 3 cloves garlic
1 T Worcestershire sauce
1 tsp Dijon mustard
1 tin (2 oz) anchovies, drained
juice of 1 lemon
salt and pepper to taste

Process olive oil and garlic in a blender or processor until garlic is finely minced. Add Worcestershire, mustard, anchovies and lemon juice, blending until creamy.

Add salt and pepper to taste.

Note: For a Caesar Salad, dress romaine lettuce and toss, add parmesan or pecorino romano cheese, and toss again.

Blue Cheese Dressing

Makes 4 cups

2 C buttermilk
1 C sour cream
1½ T prepared hot horseradish
2 tsp hot pepper sauce*
8 oz blue cheese, crumbled
salt and pepper to taste

Mix all ingredients. Refrigerate.

*We prefer using Frank's Red Hot. If using Tabasco, use 1 tsp only.

Lemon Vinaigrette

Makes 1½ cups

2 T shallots, finely chopped
1 clove garlic, finely minced
1 T lemon zest (1 to 2 lemons)
5 T lemon juice, freshly squeezed
2 T agave syrup or honey (to taste)
½ tsp salt
¼ tsp black pepper
¾ C extra-virgin olive oil

Whisk together the shallots, garlic, lemon juice, lemon zest, agave syrup, salt, and pepper in a small bowl. Drizzle oil in a slow stream into the bowl and whisk until well combined.

You can also use a small food processor to make this dressing by putting all ingredients into the processor and blend until emulsified.

Use immediately, or whisk again if left resting. Will keep in airtight container in fridge for up to 3 days.

Asian Ginger Dressing

Makes 1½ cups

2 cloves garlic, minced
1 to 2 inch piece fresh ginger, minced
½ C Orange Muscat Champagne
    vinegar*
2 T sweet Thai chili sauce
    (Nuoe cham ga)
½ tsp curry powder
⅔ C olive oil
salt and pepper to taste

Place minced garlic and ginger in a small bowl. Add vinegar, chili sauce, curry powder and whisk. Slowly drizzle oil into bowl while whisking vigorously so dressing will thicken. Add salt and pepper to taste.

*Can substitute ¼ C white balsamic vinegar combined with ¼ C orange juice.

Cranberry Vinaigrette

Makes 1½ cups

4 T cranberry juice concentrate (frozen)
2 T dried cranberries
2 cloves garlic, finely minced
4 T rice wine vinegar
1½ tsp Dijon mustard
¼ tsp coarse salt
freshly ground pepper to taste
¾ C canola oil

Whisk together all the ingredients except the oil in a small bowl. Drizzle the oil in a slow stream into the bowl and continue whisking until well combined and dressing begins to thicken.

You can also use a small food processor to make this dressing by putting all ingredients into the processor and blend until emulsified.

Use immediately, or whisk again if left resting.

Honey Mint Vinaigrette

Makes ¾ cup

2 T sherry vinegar
½ tsp coarse salt
pinch of ground pepper
4 tsp fresh mint leaves, minced
2 cloves garlic, finely minced
2 T honey
⅓ C olive oil

Whisk together all the ingredients except the olive oil in a small bowl. Drizzle the olive oil in a slow stream into the bowl and continue whisking until well combined and dressing begins to thicken.

You can also use a small food processor to make this dressing by putting all ingredients into the processor and blend until emulsified.

Use immediately, or whisk again if left resting.

The Backward Step

Before I came to Hedgebrook, I thought I was losing my mind. You know what it feels like to try to make a fist when your hand is asleep? That's how my mind felt. My journals were peppered with adjectives like *slack, scattered, foggy, fuzzy, fractured, fragmented, vague.* I spent hours on the Internet researching ADD, menopause, depression, and even Alzheimer's, the disease that claimed my mother's life. Distracted and anxious, I watched my mind for signs, all the while mourning the effect this loss of mental focus was having on my writing. I thought I'd lost the capacity to hold complex fictional worlds in my mind. I thought I would never write another novel.

When I was invited to Hedgebrook, in 2009, I almost didn't come because the cottages weren't equipped with Wi-Fi. This was almost a dealbreaker. With my lousy memory, how could I possibly write without the Internet? All my resources and references were online. My head, quite literally, was in the Cloud. But I overcame my reservations, moved into Meadow House, and started toying with a long-abandoned novel. Before I knew it, I was deep into the fictional world again, only this time, without the constant distraction of email and the Internet, I was able to stay with the story and find a way through to the end. Several years and drafts later, the novel, *A Tale for the Time Being,* is published and in the world.

What I learned at Hedgebrook was this: there is nothing wrong with my mind that a few weeks of offline writing time won't fix. This backward step is essential. Hedgebrook gave me back my writer's mind, and for that I am deeply grateful.

—Ruth Ozeki

Hedgebrook's Garden

When Nancy Nordhoff founded Hedgebrook, she understood that nurturing the land would in turn nurture us. Our forty-eight acres include cultivated gardens, pastures, ponds, meadows, park-like woodlands, and untamed second-growth forest. The garden provides abundant produce, from fresh peas and greens in the spring to autumn's squash and apples. Writers are welcome to cut flowers, sow seeds, and help gather the produce that will grace their table.

The kitchen and garden staff work together, inspiring one another to try new things. The magic happens when the freshest possible produce is harvested from the garden and brought into the kitchen, where the chefs transform it into the evening's delicious meal.

—Cathy Bruemmer, gardener

Hedgebrook's Community

Hedgebrook works to provide as much fruit and produce from our orchard and garden as possible for our residents. We would like to acknowledge and honor the other island farmers and purveyors who partner with us to complement our own garden's bounty.

We rely upon Glendale Shepherd to provide both fresh lamb and sheep cheese while Little Brown Farm provides fresh goat milk and goat cheese. Our farm fresh eggs are provided from Fox Hollow Farm as well as Whidbey Green Goods. Langley Vineyard Farm raises our red Angus beef while Stevens Family Farm provides our pork. Both Screaming Banshee Bread and Tree Top Bakery provide fresh baked breads while Grain Shadow Co-op and Whidbey Island Prairie Grains provide locally grown grains and flour for our kitchen's needs. Local Whidbey fisherman Steve Mitchell keeps us stocked with Bristol Bay sockeye salmon and family run Sylver Fishing Company provides the incomparable Alaskan spot prawns. Sea Breeze Seafood provides year-round resources for other fish and seafood.

Other farm fresh produce is procured from Greenbank Farm, Pam's Place Produce, Prairie Bottom Farm, Quail Run Farm, Rosehip Farm & Garden, Willowood Farm, and Whidbey Green Goods.

Our signature coffee blend, Dark Pond Coffee, is provided by our roaster in the woods, Mukilteo Coffee Roasters, and our two signature Hedgebrook Wines, Meadow House White and Cedar Deep Red, are vinted by local Whidbey Island Vineyard and Winery.

Hedgebrook Staff

Amy Wheeler, Executive Director
Vito Zingarelli, Residency Director
M. Louise McKay, Director of External Relations
Liz Engelman, Alumnae Relations Coordinator
Katie Woodzick, External Relations Manager
Denise Barr, House Chef
Cathy Bruemmer, Gardener

Billy Pape, Facilities Manager
Kathryn Preiss, Residency Associate
Nancy Bardue, Operations Coordinator
Kathy Watson, Head Housekeeper
Stephanie Zea, Bookkeeper
Ashley and Lance Leasure, OrangeGerbera
   organizational development

Hedgebrook Board of Directors

Shauna Woods, President
Mary Willis, Vice President
Grace Nordhoff, Treasurer
Abigail Carter, Secretary
Donna Hall

Pramila Jayapal
Sarah Lapido Manyika
Ruthann Martin
Ann Medlock
Elizabeth Rudolf

Creative Advisory Council

Gloria Steinem, Co-chair
Carolyn Forché, Co-chair
Nassim Assefi
Carole DeSanti
Eve Ensler
Karen Joy Fowler
Elizabeth George
Mary Gordon
Suheir Hammad
Pramila Jayapal

Sarah Jones
Ellen McLaughlin
Honor Moore
Holly Morris
Naomi Shihab Nye
Ruth Ozeki
Robin Swicord
Monique Truong
Sarah Waters

The recipes in this book have been lovingly created by the chefs of Hedgebrook.

Denise

Vegan Granola

Double Ginger Cookies

Chewy Fruit Cookies

Ginger Pumpkin Bread

Banana Cardamom Bread

Baked French Toast

Chard Frittata

Clam Chowder

Carrot Ginger Orange Soup

Tomato Coconut Soup

Chicken Tortilla Soup

Hot and Sour Soup

Quinoa Apricot Almond Salad

Nana's Potato Salad

Cioppino

Grilled Salmon with Asian Cilantro Sauce

Cauliflower Mac & Cheese

Vietnamese Noodle Salad Bowls

Vegetarian Enchiladas

Braised Brussels Sprouts with Pancetta

Fennel Gratin

Hummus

Eggplant Caponata

Gravlax with Grapefruit

Smoked Salmon Cheesecake

Italian Chicken Stew

Vegetarian Lasagna

Apple Raspberry Crisp

Chipotle Brownies

Cheesecake

Rhubarb Cake

Dijon Balsamic Vinaigrette

Caesar Dressing

Blue Cheese Dressing

Asian Ginger Dressing

Julie

Chocolate Shortbread

Lavender Shortbread

Toasted Sesame Cookies

Candied Almonds

Gingered Pecans

Blueberry Scones

Savory Galette

Spinach Pie

Zucchini Potato Frittata

Baked Chile Rellenos

Zucchini Bisque

Ginger Broth with Sweet Potatoes

Tuscan Kale and Apple Salad

Beet and Fennel Salad

Shrimp and Mango Salad

Asparagus Chicken Salad

Grilled Salmon with Cucumber and Fennel Relish

Sicilian Snapper

Turkey Burgers

Zucchini Fritters

Curried Cauliflower and Potatoes

Sweet Potato Fries with Yogurt Lime Sauce

Parsnips and Carrots

Seaweed Salad

Asparagus Gruyere Tart

Slow-Roasted Tomatoes

Crostini

Baked Brie

Figs with Prosciutto

Full Moonssaka

Lamb Curry

Applesauce Cake

Carrot Cake

Pear Galette

Salted Caramel Ice Cream

Honey Lavender Ice Cream

Raspberry Moscato Sorbet

Buttermilk Dressing

Lemon Vinaigrette

Cranberry Vinaigrette

Honey Mint Vinaigrette

Jennifer

Spicy Caramel Corn

Tomato Tart

Curried Chicken Salad

Roast Chicken

Lemon Polenta Cake

Anne

Vegan Pumpkin Bread

Anne's Muffins

Jonni

Tofu with Napa Cabbage Salad

Stuffed Mushrooms

Elizabeth

Chocolate Ganache Tarts

Vanilla Bean Panna Cotta

Acknowledgments

This cookbook is a labor of love. In the deepest sense, its contents echo what happens at Hedgebrook. Love and thanks to our chefs Denise and Julie who have devoted countless hours to creating this cookbook, in the same way they go about preparing meals for our writers-in-residence: with thoughtful attention to what each writer needs to fuel her creative process. Food allergies are considered and "comfort foods" are given priority. If you're gluten-free or lactose intolerant, there's always a special dessert for you - and the cookie jar is never empty. (Suffice it to say: no one goes without dessert at Hedgebrook!)

Love and thanks also goes to: Liz Engelman, our Alumnae Relations Coordinator and dramaturg-at-large, for lending her extraordinary editorial expertise; our alumnae writers who've generously contributed their stories and poems; and Kamy Wicoff and Brooke Warner at She Writes Press, who've made this cookbook their first "passion project." Thanks to their generosity, the costs of creating the book were minimal, and proceeds will benefit Hedgebrook. And to Tabitha Lahr, designer extraordinaire, who executed our vision to create something we are proud to bring to our community.

Thanks to: our guest chefs Jennifer Ruemping, Anne Huggins, Jonni Reed and Elizabeth Frediani for sharing their recipes; Jeanne Brennan, Pam Eimers, Lianna Gilman, Sue Kramer, Liza Jane vonRosenstiel, Megan Woo, and Vito Zingarelli for each sharing one of their personal favorites; Cecilia Hae-Jin Lee and Valerie Easton for their advice and guidance in the early stages of this project; and to all of the chefs who have graced Hedgebrook's kitchen over the past 25 years.

And finally, love and thanks to Nancy Nordhoff for creating a home-away-from-home for women writers, and instilling "radical hospitality" into the very heart of Hedgebrook. Over a quarter century, that simple act has grown into a global community of women writers empowered and transformed by that focus. The impact of this quiet place will be felt for centuries to come.

Contributor Bios

NASSIM ASSEFI is an Iranian-American novelist, women's health doctor, TEDGlobal Fellow, and civic activist. She is the author of *Aria* and *Say I Am You* (forthcoming). Recent honors include a Woman of Courage award by the University of Washington, Top 40 Under 40 Feminist by Feminist Press, and being named one of the best doctors by Seattle Metropolitan Magazine, but none compare to the gift of being a Hedgebrook writer in residence. She is a member of Hedgebrook's Creative Advisory Council.

Photo credit: Niku Kashef

ERICA BAUERMEISTER is the bestselling author of three novels: *The School of Essential Ingredients, Joy For Beginners,* and *The Lost Art of Mixing.* She is also the co-author of *500 Great Books by Women: A Reader's Guide* and *Let's Hear It For the Girls: 375 Great Books for Readers 2-14.* She lives in Port Townsend, Washington.

Photo credit: Susan Doupe

CLAIRE DEDERER's bestselling memoir *Poser: My Life in Twenty-Three Yoga Poses* came out in January 2011 and has been translated into eleven languages. Claire is a longtime contributor to *The New York Times.* Her articles have appeared in *Vogue, Real Simple, The Nation, New York, Yoga Journal,* on Slate and Salon, and in newspapers across the country. Her writing has encompassed criticism, reporting, and the personal essay.

Photo credit: D'Arcy McGrath

VALERIE EASTON is a weekly columnist for *Pacific Northwest Magazine* of *The Seattle Times* and for Crosscut.com. She's the author of five gardening books, including *The New Low-Maintenance Garden,* which was chosen by Amazon.com as one of the Ten Best Home and Garden Books for 2009. Valerie blogs at www.valeaston.com and teaches yoga in Langley, Washington, on Whidbey Island.

Photo credit: Katherine Easton

CAROLYN FORCHÉ is the award-winning poet and author of *Gathering the Tribes, The Country Between Us,* and *The Angel of History,* and the editor of the anthology *Against Forgetting: Twentieth-Century Poetry of Witness.* Recently she was presented with the Edita and Ira Morris Hiroshima Foundation Award for Peace and Culture in Stockholm. She serves as co-chair of Hedgebrook's Creative Advisory Council.

Photo credit: Don J. Usher

RUTH FORMAN is the author of three award-winning books: poetry collections *We Are the Young Magicians* (Beacon, 1993) and *Renaissance* (Beacon, 1997) and the children's book *Young Cornrows Callin Out the Moon* (Children's Book Press, 2007). She frequently collaborates on film, music, dance, theatre, art, and media projects. Her latest collection is *Prayers Like Shoes* (Whit Press, 2009). Ms. Forman currently lives in Washington, D.C.

Photo credit: Christine Bennett

KAREN JOY FOWLER is the author of six novels and three short story collections, including *Sarah Canary* and *The Jane Austen Book Club.* Her collection *What I Didn't See* recently won the 2010 World Fantasy Award and her new novel, *We Are All Completely Beside Ourselves,* was released in May of 2013. She is a member of Hedgebrook's Creative Advisory Council.

Photo credit: Brett Hall Jones

JANE HAMILTON has written several novels, lives in Wisconsin, and in her spare time dreams of mealtime at Hedgebrook.

Photo Credit: Kevin Horan

ANNIE RACHELE LANZILLOTTO is the author of *L is for Lion: An Italian Bronx Butch Freedom Memoir* (SUNY Press, 2013) and the book of poetry *Schistsong* (Bordighera Press, 2013). Lanzillotto is the songwriter/vocalist on the album *Blue Pill* by the Annie Lanzillotto Band (StreetCry Productions, 2010). As a guest artist, she teaches master classes in solo theater to the Apprentice Company at the Actors Theatre of Louisville as well as theater outreach at Sarah Lawrence College. www.annielanzillotto.com.

Photo credit: Carolina Kroon

ELLEN MCLAUGHLIN's plays have received numerous national and international productions as well as several awards. Plays include *Iphigenia and Other Daughters, Tongue of a Bird, Ajax in Iraq,* and *Septimus and Clarissa.* Producers include The Public Theater, New York Theater Workshop, The Guthrie Theater, and The Almeida Theater, London. She is also an actor, known best for originating the role of the Angel in Tony Kushner's *Angels in America.* She is a member of Hedgebrook's Creative Advisory Council.

Photo credit: T. Charles Erickson

THAO NGUYEN is a folk singer-songwriter out of Virginia. After picking up her guitar at the age of twelve, Thao began performing and recording as a pop-country duo with a high school friend. In 2005 she recorded *Like The Linen,* her first full-length album. Thao released her second album, *We Brave Bee Stings and All,* in 2008. Her band, The Get Down Stay Down, now consists of Nguyen, Willis Thompson, Adam Thompson, and Frank Stewart. Thao continues to perform as a soloist on occasion.

Photo credit: Lauren Tabak

RUTH OZEKI is a filmmaker-turned-novelist-turned-Zen-Buddhist-priest and is the author of *My Year of Meats, All Over Creation,* and *A Tale for the Time Being.* She is on the advisory editorial board of the Asian American Literary Review and is a member of Hedgebrook's Creative Advisory Council.

Photo credit: Kris Krug

RAHNA REIKO RIZZUTO is the author of *Hiroshima in the Morning,* a National Book Critics Circle Finalist, an Asian American Literary Award Finalist, a Dayton Literary Peace Prize Nominee, and the winner of the Grub Street National Book Award. Her novel *Why She Left Us* won an American Book Award in 2000. She is also a recipient of the U.S./Japan Creative Artist Fellowship, funded by the National Endowment for the Arts. Her website is www.rahnareikorizzuto.com.

Photo credit: John Searcy

SUSAN B. ANTHONY SOMERS-WILLETT is the author of two books of poetry—*Roam* (Crab Orchard Award, 2006) and *Quiver* (University of Georgia Press, 2009)—as well as a book of criticism, *The Cultural Politics of Slam Poetry* (University of Michigan Press, 2009). Her poetry and essays have been featured by *The Iowa Review, Poets & Writers, Virginia Quarterly Review,* and *The New Yorker.* She lives in Austin, Texas, with her daughter Elizabeth Cady.

Photo credit: Susan B. Anthony Somers-Willett

GLORIA STEINEM is a writer, lecturer, editor, and feminist activist. Gloria is currently at work on *Road to the Heart: America as if Everyone Mattered,* about her more than fifty years on the road as a feminist organizer, which has primarily been written at Hedgebrook. Her bestsellers include *Revolution from Within: A Book of Self-Esteem, Outrageous Acts and Everyday Rebellions,* and *Moving Beyond Words.* As founder and co-chair of Hedgebrook's Creative Advisory Council, Gloria works closely with staff and board to raise Hedgebrook's profile and guide its vision.

Photo credit: Tom Marks

SAMANTHA THORNHILL has been invited to perform poetry on stages across the United States as well as South Africa, Bermuda, Hungary, and her homeland of Trinidad and Tobago. After receiving her master's in Fine Arts in poetry from the University of Virginia, Samantha moved to New York City, where she currently serves as writer in residence at the Bronx Academy of Letters and teaches poetry to actors in training at the Juilliard School.

Photo credit: Derek Jones

Born in Saigon in 1968, MONIQUE TRUONG is a novelist based in Brooklyn. Her first novel, *The Book of Salt* (2003), was a national bestseller and was named a New York Times Notable Fiction Book, among other honors. Her second novel, *Bitter in the Mouth* (2010), received the Rosenthal Family Foundation Award from the American Academy of Arts and Letters and was named a best fiction book of the year by Barnes & Noble and Hudson Booksellers. She lives to eat and, sometimes, to write. She is a member of Hedgebrook's Creative Advisory Council.

Photo credit: Susanna Kekkonen

GAIL TSUKIYAMA is the author of seven novels, including *Women of the Silk* and *The Samurai's Garden.* She has been the recipient of the Academy of American Poets Award, the PEN/Oakland Josephine Miles Award for Literary Excellence, and the Asia Pacific Leadership Award from the Center of the Pacific Rim and the Ricci Institute. A resident of the San Francisco Bay Area, she has taught at San Francisco State University; University of California, Berkeley; and Mills College. Her latest novel, *A Hundred Flowers,* was published by St. Martin's Press in August 2012.

Photo credit: Kevin Horan

LIZ ENGELMAN is a freelance dramaturg who is currently splitting her time between Whidbey Island, WA and Ely, MN, where she is the Alumnae Relations Coordinator of Hedgebrook, and is the founder and director of Tofte Lake Center at Norm's Fish Camp, a creative retreat in the Boundary Waters of Minnesota. Liz has worked as a Literary Director/Dramaturg on the development of new plays at festivals and regional theatres across the country. Liz is the co-editor of several collections of plays, a book on playwriting exercises, two volumes of monologues, and a collection of Hedgebrook plays, co-edited with Christine Sumption and published by Whit Press.

Photo credit: Nancy Bardue

Chef Bios

 ELIZABETH FREDIANI wears many professional hats—over thirty-five years as an energy practitioner, meditation instructor, astrologer, and recently, author of *and then there is pastry chef*. Her training at Le Cordon Bleu and Ewald Notter's confectionery school indulged her life-long passion for creating and eating delectable sweets—and now she indulges the writers' passions for all things chocolate.

Photo credit: A.T. Birmingham Young

 ANNE HUGGINS considers Hedgebrook her dream job. Anne found Hedgebrook just as it was celebrating its tenth birthday and has since loved being part of supporting women's voices. She splits her time between Whidbey and Patagonia, Arizona, where she explores relationships with children, food, art, writing, and outdoor adventures.

Photo credit: Nancy Bardue

 JONNI REED is one of many domestic divas balancing a creative life here on Whidbey Island. As an active interior designer, oil painter, and catering cook, she has found many ways to share her love of color, texture, and flavor. With much pleasure feeding people, Jonni enjoys her stints making meals in the cozy Hedgebrook kitchen.

Photo credit: Sarah Fosmo

 JENNIFER RUEMPING owns and runs an interior design firm in Seattle, highlighting beauty and function in everything she does. Cooking is a passion for her, and she loves to create dishes that let the ingredients shine. Her motto in the kitchen and in life: Bring comfort and sophistication to the way we live today and every day.

Photo credit: Rebecca Rober

About the Chefs/Authors

DENISE BARR has lived on Whidbey Island for fifteen years with her husband and their many inspiring animals. She has always been involved in the arts community, and for twenty-five years she has been teaching and creating jewelry with galleries throughout the western United States. Denise treasures the creative and nuturing environment that is Hedgebrook. As house chef for the past five years, she considers it an honor to prepare the meal and join the writers for dinner. Everyone has a story to tell, a wonderful gift to bring to the table.

JULIE ROSTEN is a native Seattleite, who moved to Whidbey Island 12 years ago to seek a life-style closer to nature. Educated in the arts, she has spent a lifetime fostering the creative efforts of those she meets. From providing art classes to children in the '80s, to opening a gallery showcasing young emerging artists in the '90s, to managing the private businesses of artists on the island, she has found her true calling as a guest chef at Hedgebrook nurturing the writers. Her palette is multicultural and her dishes are artfully prepared with the love and gratitude for everything that contributes to the meal: from the seed savers, farmers, ranchers, poultry women, fisherwomen, mushroom foragers and seaweed harvesters to the eaters that sit at her table.

Photo credit (on opposite page): Michael Stadler

Photographer Bios

MICHAEL STADLER has always been an observer by nature, standing back and looking deeper into what lay in front of him, and has always felt there was a place within our world that could be seen if it was just looked at closer and longer. Michael's studio offers many services from wedding coverage, portraiture, and product photography. He grew up just down the street from Hedgebrook, where he is now raising his own children. www.stadlerstudio.com.

Photo credit: Michael Stadler

M.J. ALEXANDER is a writer and photographer who documents people and places of the American West, with an emphasis on the overlooked and underappreciated. Her work has been featured on national magazine covers and exhibited here and abroad. She is author and illustrator of two books: *Salt of the Red Earth,* portraits of and interviews with 100 Oklahoma centenarians, and *Portrait of a Generation: Sons and Daughters of the Red Earth,* winner of a 2011 Oklahoma Book Award and a gold medal from the Independent Publishers Awards. Her fine-art portraits have been featured in 15 solo shows since 2006.

Photo credit: Alexander Knight

Photo Credits

MJ ALEXANDER: mailbox, cover; Nancy Nordhoff book flap; Amy Timberlake, p. xiv; Randy Sue Coburn, p. 44; Uchechi Kalu, p. 68; Nassim Assefi, p. 114; p. 174

JOANN GRAMBUSH: p. 124

HEDGEBROOK STAFF: garden apple, cover; Cathy, cover; p. 10; p. 22; p. 26; p. 40; (left to right) Danai Gurira, Carolyn Forché, Samantha Thornhill, p. 58; Cathy Bruemmer, p. 62; p. 74; (clockwise) Denise Barr, Rebekah Anne Bloyd, Vito Zingarelli, Carolyn Forche, Monique Truong, Dael Orlandersmith, p. 76; p. 88; p. 136; p. 146; p. 172; p. 180

WILLA KVETA: p. xvi; p. 6

TOM MARKS: cottage blue door, cover; Gloria Steinem, p. viii; Amy Wheeler, p. x; (left to right) Frances Richey, Kimberly Foote, Maggie Dubris, Anene Ejikeme, Gloria Steinem, Nancy Pearl, Shasta Grant, Randy Sue Coburn, Amy Wheeler, Nassim Assefi, Claudia Mauro, Holly Hughes, p. xii; Monique Truong, Suheir Hammad, p. xviii; p. 16; p. 52; p. 164; p. 170

RUSSELL SPARKMAN: p. 182

MICHAEL STADLER: pear tart, cover; cioppino, cover; p.2; p. 12; p. 28; p. 32; p. 34; p. 36; p. 46; p. 50; p. 56; p. 60; p. 66; p. 72; p. 78; p. 86; p. 92; p. 98; p. 102; p. 104; p. 106; p. 112; p. 118; p. 120; p. 128; p. 132; p. 144; p. 154; p. 158; p. 162; p. 168; p. 176; Hedgebrook Staff (clockwise) M. Louise McKay (with baby Tebr), Cathy Bruemmer, Amy Wheeler, Katie Woodzick, Vito Zingarelli, Billy Pape, Liz Engelman, Julie Rosten, Kathy Watson, Denise Barr, Kathryn Preiss, p. 184

MARY TANG: p. 96

ABI TSCHETTER: p. 4; Julie, p. 20; Gail Tsukiyama, Ruth Ozeki, p. 82; (clockwise) Karen Joy Fowler, Gail Tsukiyama, Jane Hamilton, Dorothy Allison, Ruth Ozeki, Elizabeth George, p. 110; Denise Barr, Jonni Reed, p. 130; (clockwise) Ruth Ozeki, Karen Joy Fowler, Dorothy Allison, Denise Barr, Jane Hamilton, Gail Tsukiyama, Elizabeth George, p. 150

DORIT ZINGARELLI: Denise and Julie, cover; p. 138

Index